WHY
DO I DO THAT?

Also by Joseph Burgo

Non-fiction

The Narcissist You Know
Defending Yourself Against Extreme Narcissists in an All-About-Me World

Building Self Esteem
How Learning from Shame Helps Us to Grow

Fiction

Grim
Dark Fairy Tales for the Psychologically Minded

The Lights of Barbrin

Vacillian
Book One of the Illuminariad

WHY
DO I DO THAT?

PSYCHOLOGICAL DEFENSE
MECHANISMS AND THE HIDDEN WAYS
THEY SHAPE OUR LIVES

JOSEPH BURGO, Ph.D.

NEW RISE PRESS
CHAPEL HILL NC

ISBN: 978-0-988-44312-9

New Rise Press ◄╫
1818 Martin Luther King Jr. Blvd.
Chapel Hill, NC 27514

www.afterpsychotherapy.com

To R. and S., and all my clients these many years.

Table of Contents

Introduction

I began my training as a psychotherapist more than 30 years ago and I've spent most of my career since then in private practice, working with adults who came to me because of unbearable anxiety or depression, unhappiness in their marriage, an eating disorder, shame or self-loathing, compulsive behavior – for many different reasons but each one involving deep pain. This book represents my effort to distill that experience and what I've learned into a useful guide for people who aren't necessarily in therapy and may not be able to afford it.

I view human nature and psychology from a *psychodynamic perspective*: I believe that for each and every one of us, hidden aspects of our mental life remain outside of awareness and are thus *unconscious*. As a psychodynamic psychotherapist, my job is to acquaint clients with those unknown parts, and one of the primary ways I do this is by helping them to understand the *psychological defense mechanisms* that keep painful emotions, thoughts and fears outside of awareness.

Those defense mechanisms are the subject matter of this book: how they function, the painful elements of human experience they typically exclude from awareness, the reasons why we rely upon them and the potentially great benefits of acknowledging and facing the unconscious pain that lies behind them. Psychological defense mechanisms are a universal and necessary part of human psychology; they protect and help us to navigate the more difficult aspects of human experience, but often, they stand in the way of growth and satisfaction. Rigid or deeply entrenched defenses may prevent us from getting what we truly need in our relationships, from leading a rich emotional life and living in ways that promote authentic self-esteem. This book will help you recognize your own defense mechanisms at work and determine when you need to move beyond them in order to grow.

Although confronting pain may seem like a difficult chore, it can also be a liberating and exciting experience. What could be more fascinating than to probe your own depths, to recognize the rich psychological complexity of your friends, family members and acquaintances, to view human relationships with deeper understanding? After so many years in practice, I still love my work and find other people endlessly fascinating; I hope this book will impart some of that enthusiasm to you, as well.

My aim is to explain the central concepts and strategies of psychodynamic psychotherapy as I practice it, adapting them to a course of individual self-exploration outside of treatment. *Why Do I Do That?* begins by discussing the nature and purpose of psychological defense mechanisms, as well as those difficult aspects of the human experience that typically give rise to them (Part I). In the long middle section of the book (Part II), I take a closer look at the most important defense mechanisms, with exercises to help readers recognize their own defenses at work and identify unconscious feelings behind them. Part III concludes with several chapters that discuss ways to disarm those defenses and cope more effectively with our most difficult emotions.

In the coming pages, I'll spend a great deal of time discussing and helping readers become aware of pain which they may have a difficult time facing. The experience of reading this book, especially if you engage fully in the exercises, will be neither easy nor comfortable, but I'm confident that if you persevere, you'll see the benefits of greater self-awareness. *Why Do I Do That?* may help you to get more of what you need from your relationships, to develop a vivid but manageable emotional life, to know yourself better – your strengths as well as your limitations – and thus to develop realistic expectations for yourself that promote genuine self-esteem.

Just as clients in psychotherapy can't face the full extent of their pain all at once – *nobody* could do that – you probably won't be able to absorb all of the insights offered by this book in one go. You may need to read it more than once, or tackle a few chapters now and read the rest later, after you've had time to integrate what you've learned. Real growth occurs little by little, often over long periods of time. While it's important to persevere and not turn away whenever you feel threatened, don't drive yourself too hard or expect more of yourself than you can manage. Each new bit of self-awareness, each step forward has its value.

Also bear in mind that nobody ever gets beyond his defense mechanisms and ceases to rely upon them. Although I'm a therapist, the author of this book and your presumptive guide in this venture of self-exploration, I continue to confront and wrestle with my own defense mechanisms every day of my life. One of the primary messages of this book is that our sensitive emotional issues will continue to pose challenges for us throughout our lives, though with time and effort, we will navigate them more easily and with greater self-confidence.

In other words, the process of confronting pain and struggling with the often difficult memories associated with it is a challenge *for everyone*. As you work your way through the book and exercises, remember that in some larger sense, although it may not always be of immediate comfort, other people engaged in the same journey are struggling, too.

∗   ∗   ∗

The psychodynamic perspective is rooted in the work of Sigmund Freud. As a young psychoanalyst, I used to teach a year-long course covering all 24 volumes of his work–a standard part of the curriculum at most psychoanalytic training institutes throughout the world. Freud has fallen out of favor during the past 50 years, largely because he failed to understand female sexuality and held some views about women that today would be considered misogynistic or patronizing; he's widely considered obsolete and passé.

Despite this view, many of his revolutionary insights have been incorporated into our culture as basic assumptions. Even people who dismiss Freud often accept many of the core tenets of psychoanalysis without realizing it. Our culture has been profoundly and forever changed by his pioneering work.

Since Freud died in 1939, many influential theorists have extended and corrected his ideas. I'll be referring to some of them as I go along, but more often than not I'll be referring to Freud. By the end of this book, I hope you'll have a deeper appreciation for his contribution to our culture, seeing in him, as I do, a revolutionary genius who helped shape the way we all think about ourselves and other people every day, even when we don't realize it.

PART I

Understanding Our Psychological Defense Mechanisms

ONE

The "Me" I Don't Know

...he hath ever but slenderly known himself.
— King Lear, Act I, Scene i

At one time or another, most of us go through an experience when we feel, talk or behave in ways that take us by surprise, when we suddenly see that something unrecognized has been going on "behind the scenes." What seems like a minor incident may set us off and we suddenly realize we've been feeling something intense for a while without being aware of it.

Your partner has been putting in long hours at work and you've gladly picked up the slack at home. *Poor guy, he's working so hard.* Then when you ask him to stop at the dry cleaner on his way into the office and he hesitates before saying *yes*, you snap, "Never mind! I'll do it myself!"

At the last minute, your friend calls to cancel plans—"Something's come up...do you mind?"—and you feel surprisingly upset. Over the years, you've made generous allowance for this kind of inconsideration. Now you realize that you haven't gotten over the fact that she forgot your birthday last year. You see clearly what you've always known but didn't want to face: she has other friendships she values more highly than yours.

Your mother died six months ago after a protracted illness. At the time, you felt you'd done most of your grieving during her illness and that when death finally put an end to her suffering, it came almost as a relief. One evening, as you're watching a sad movie, you suddenly begin to sob, realizing how much you miss your mom.

We usually go through life believing that our conscious experience of ourselves is the beginning and end of who we are; in truth, important parts of our emotional lives may remain hidden from us. This is not a new idea. At least as far back as Shakespeare's time (see the quotation that heads this chapter), students of human nature have observed that some people know themselves better than others do.

Jane Austen's novels are full of characters who come to understand how certain attitudes or passions have blinded them to their own true nature. In *Pride and Prejudice*, after finally acknowledging the truth in Darcy's letter, Elizabeth Bennett thinks: "Till this moment, I never knew myself." Throughout the history of the novel, authors such as Vladimir Nabokov and Ford Madox Ford have used unreliable narrators to portray men and women out-of-touch with some truth at the heart of their emotional lives.

The term "subconscious mind" was coined by the 18th century German philosopher Sir Christopher Riegel, introduced into English by Samuel Taylor Coleridge and taken up by Sigmund Freud more than a century ago as the corner stone of his psychoanalytic theories. Since then, the notion of an unconscious[1] part of the mind, remote from awareness, has entered the cultural heritage, permeating our shared understanding of the self and its landscape.

It's fairly common to speak of a "Freudian slip," for example – a mix-up in language that reveals something the speaker didn't consciously intend to say. You may be familiar with this example from Woody Allen's film *Annie Hall*: the title character has started intensive psychoanalysis and says, "I don't think I mind analysis at all. The only question is: Will

---

[1] In everyday language, many people refer to it as the "the subconscious," though strictly speaking, the correct term is "the unconscious" and the way I'll be referring to it throughout this book.

it change my wife?" The Freudian slip is a favorite trope in Hollywood, played for laughs in movies such as the Austen Powers series, *Bruce Almighty* and *Liar, Liar*.

Many people infer unconscious motives behind certain actions such as "forgetting" an unwelcome obligation or chore: it's not that the person deliberately neglected to do what he or she had promised; rather, the act of forgetting betrayed a reluctance to follow through. I doubt that many married people whose spouse "forgot" their anniversary would regard the lapse as having absolutely no meaning.

We often believe we know things about other people that they themselves can't see. When co-workers go out for lunch together and talk about another colleague, one of them might say something like: "I should've known better because she really can't take criticism. She thinks she's so perfect." A group of old friends might discuss an absent buddy and his new girlfriend: "Can't he see she's the same domineering type all over again? Exactly like his mother!" Listening to a friend talk about his plans for turning over *yet another* new leaf, you may privately have thought, *Oh stop lying to yourself.*

While we assume we have special insight into people around us, we're likely to resent it if someone presumes the same thing in relation to us. The possibility that we're unable to recognize something about ourselves that other people can see is an extremely unpleasant one for most people. If a friend suggests as much, we'll insist that our slip of the tongue was a chemical glitch, with no meaning whatsoever; that we forgot the dinner date because we were incredibly stressed at work; that omitting a name from the guest list was a simple oversight and had nothing to do with the way that person snubbed us last year at the Christmas party.

Sometimes we *do* forget because we're over-burdened at the office. Sometimes that slip of the tongue really has no meaning. But often, oversights and slips reveal something at work that we're not aware of and may not want to acknowledge, even to ourselves.

The fact that we're able to recognize unconscious motivations in other people more readily than in ourselves makes perfect sense when you consider the nature of the unconscious, why certain thoughts and feelings remain unconscious and others don't. According to the many psychodynamic theorists who have written about this, from Freud onward, the unconscious carries all the thoughts and feelings we either find too painful to bear, or which conflict with our morality and values and undermine our self-image. In other words, we don't *want* to know about the contents of our unconscious. If we did want to know, those thoughts and feelings wouldn't be unconscious in the first place.

So how do we manage to avoid encountering those parts of ourselves we find too difficult to bear? How is it possible for an aspect of our personality to remain a stranger to us when other people can see it?

This is where *psychological defense mechanisms* (also called *psychological defenses* or simply *defenses)* come into play. Our defense mechanisms are invisible methods by which we exclude unacceptable thoughts and feelings from awareness. In the process, they subtly distort our perceptions of reality – in both our personal relationships and the emotional terrain within us. This book will be devoted to describing those defense mechanisms, understanding how they operate and learning to identify them within ourselves. It will also teach more effective ways to cope with and express what resides in the unconscious: when our defenses become too rigid or entrenched, they may prevent us from leading a full and satisfying emotional life.

*   *   *

During my college years when I was deeply depressed and sought professional help, like many people entering psychotherapy I assumed that my therapist would teach me new methods or techniques in order to resolve my difficulties. To my surprise (and often discomfort), I soon learned that instead, he'd listen very carefully to everything I said and then tell me something entirely unexpected, about some aspect of my emotional life that I hadn't been able to see. Although I rejected many of the things he told me, and sometimes felt deeply angered by them, over time I inadvertently brought him enough examples to validate his insights so that I came to accept them as true.

During the 30 years since I became a psychotherapist, I've worked in the same way. I listen to the people who come for help and hear many things they don't consciously intend to tell me—about unbearable feelings of need, anger too frightening to acknowledge, poisonous envy or jealousy, debilitating shame and other emotions so intense my clients can't stand to let them in. I try to help them understand their own defense mechanisms—the unconscious ways they ward off parts of their experience which they find too painful to bear. I also show them how a particular defense often stops them from getting what they truly need or from taking the best care of themselves and their personal relationships.

For here is the problem inherent in psychological defenses: while they're necessary and useful, for each and every one of us, in coping with the inevitable pain that goes with being human, when they become too deeply entrenched, they may prevent us from accessing important emotions we *need* to face.

On the one hand, temporarily numbing yourself to overwhelming grief may help you weather the loss of a loved one; on the other, blinding yourself to the emotional poverty of your childhood might mean you can't see how that past plays a role in your unhappy marriage. Shutting out the awareness that we're all heading toward death allows us to function on a daily basis and get on with our lives; engaging in high-risk behavior because you unconsciously believe you're invulnerable, not mortal like everyone else, can have tragic results.

By excluding large parts of our emotional experience, we deplete ourselves, diminishing our strength and ability to cope in the world. Anger, for example, can motivate us to make important changes in our lives—to leave an unhealthy relationship with a selfish partner or end a one-sided friendship, to protect ourselves in the face of mistreatment.

Admitting the guilt and regret we feel about the way we behaved can help us make it up to someone we care for.

By diverting or misdirecting the expression of some of our strongest passions, our defense mechanisms often lead us to act in ways that don't get us what we truly need; instead, they may be self-defeating or even self-destructive.

Worst of all, psychological defenses may exclude or misdirect parts of our emotional life that we need for effective relationships – not just romantic ones but those with our family members and close friends, or with our colleagues at work. If you block out the awareness of your own needs, you're unable to develop true intimacy. When you "swallow" your anger or unhappiness by compulsive over-eating, you're not motivated to do anything about the cause of those feelings, whether at home, with your friends or at work. People who habitually withdraw when someone else expresses an emotion that frightens them will develop limited, unsatisfying relationships that pose no threat.

Along the way, this book will apply everything we learn about defense mechanisms to an understanding of their impact on our relationships. We'll look at the role they play in those unhappy patterns we can't seem to shake, the inability to achieve closeness and commitment, recurring difficulties in the workplace, friendships that break down, difficult communications with our parents or our children, and so on.

Our final goal will be learning to disarm those defense mechanisms, the ones that prevent satisfying contact with important people in our world, and to find more effective ways to express what lies in the unconscious. Not all defense mechanisms need to be disarmed, nor must everything that resides in the unconscious be faced; but when our defenses become too rigid or entrenched, profoundly interfering with our relationships, we need to develop more conscious and flexible methods to help us cope.

What is a Psychological Defense Mechanism?

Like the notion of an unconscious mind, the idea of psychological defenses has entered the mainstream, coloring our understanding of human nature. Nearly everyone understands what it means to appear *defensive* or to react *defensively*. We use those words to describe people's behavior when they don't want to admit the truth of something said about them.

"Have you noticed how defensive Jeff gets whenever you bring up the subject of his brother? You know he has to feel guilty about what happened at his wedding."

We recognize that the person is trying to ward off something painful or unpleasant he or she doesn't want to face. We owe this understanding of defensiveness to the earliest work of Sigmund Freud.

Freud began writing about the concept of psychological defenses in the 1890s, most notably in his famous early work, *Studies on Hysteria* (1895), which he co-authored with Josef Breuer.[2] Freud wrote in German, of course, and the word he used to describe this mental phenomenon was *abwehr*, more accurately translated as a "warding off" or "fending off" rather than "defense."

We're stuck with many unfortunate translations of Freud's terminology. For example, he used the everyday word *das Ich* (the "I" or "me") when he wrote about the self and the conscious mind; instead of using the same everyday kind of language in English, his translators imported the word *ego* from Latin, giving it a weightier, more "scientific" sound. As a young discipline often attacked and ridiculed by the medical establishment of its day, psychoanalysis wanted very much to be taken seriously.

Freud's idea is a simple one, and not as machine-like as the unfortunate English term *defense mechanism* makes it sound. According to

---

[2]Josef Breuer and Sigmund Freud. Studies on hysteria. *Standard Edition of the Complete Psychological Works of Sigmund Freud*, **3**. (London: The Hogarth Press, 1953). All references to this edition will hereafter use the abbreviation "S.E," followed by the volume number.

Freud, sometimes when we're confronted with an idea or feeling that we find too painful or morally unacceptable, we ward it off, pushing it into the unconscious. It's not a deliberate decision; it happens outside of awareness, in ways that are often automatic. Freud began to articulate this view toward the end of the 19th century.

His original view of the nature and function of psychological defenses is widely accepted by most psychodynamic thinkers and therapists today, though many other writers have contributed to and expanded our understanding since Freud first introduced the concept – Alfred Adler, Anna Freud and Melanie Klein to name but a few. The simplest and least theoretical explanation comes from the British psychoanalyst Donald Meltzer who, throughout his work, holds that all defense mechanisms are essentially *lies we tell ourselves to evade pain*.[3]

This view of the nature and function of defense mechanisms makes it easier to connect them to our personal experience. Everyone can sympathize with the desire to avoid pain. We all understand how easy it is to deceive ourselves when to face the truth will hurt badly or make it difficult for us to function. Sometimes, our defense mechanisms help us to get by when to face the full truth would render life unbearable.

At other times, however, we need to confront our pain; avoiding the truth feels better for the moment, but it might only make matters worse in the long run. Here's an example using one of the most common defense mechanisms, one that everyone understands: to be *in denial* about your spouse's affair (despite the tell-tale signs) might help you avoid feeling the pain of betrayal, but it prevents you from dealing with this catastrophe in your life and all the collateral damage – to your children, your friendships, your feelings of self-worth.

Defense mechanisms operate in the here-and-now, with no thought for tomorrow. They're unthinking and reflexive; they aim only

---

[3] Meltzer developed this view of defenses from ideas implicit in the work of another British psychoanalyst, W.R. Bion.

to ward off pain this very moment and don't take into account the long-term costs of doing so. Sometimes we eventually "wake up" and face the truth. Sometimes unconscious knowledge breaks through and we realize what has been brewing unnoticed inside us for a long time. More often, we continue as we were, our defense mechanisms in place and unnoticed. Human beings are creatures of habit and change is difficult.

This book aims to instigate change by helping you to identify your typical defense mechanisms, to disarm them and develop more effective ways to deal with the truth in those cases where doing so will improve your life and your relationships.

Defense Mechanisms and Your Personality

Whenever we discuss psychological defense mechanisms one-by-one, as individual strategies, it gives the misleading impression that they're discrete techniques used in isolation—as if you were playing golf with the choice of using a wood, iron or wedge for any particular shot. In truth, we tend to develop characteristic or habitual defenses, or groups of them, and those customary ways of warding off pain play a role in shaping our entire personality.

Wilhelm Reich took up this issue in his seminal work, *Character Analysis* (1933). While English speakers today use the word *character* when talking of eccentricity or morals—"He's such a character," we might say; or, "She's a woman of fine character"—Reich used the German word *Charakter* more in the sense of "personality." He believed that one's personality or "character traits as a whole [are] a compact defense mechanism" with the same warding-off effect as any other psychological defense.[4] Such a defense shows up "in the way one typically behaves, in the manner in which one speaks, walks, and gestures; and in one's

---

[4]Wilhelm Reich. *Charakteranalyse* (1933). In English: (New York: Farrar, Strauss and Giroux, 1972) p.48.

characteristic habits (how one smiles or sneers...*how* one is polite and *how* one is aggressive)."[5]

So if people would describe you as an exceptionally nice person who never gets upset or angry, that description would likely tell us something about your characteristic defense mechanisms. If you're an assertive person who tends to dominate a situation, shouting down other people or badgering them until they agree with you—that would suggest an entirely different set of defenses. Your habitual ways of interacting with the important people in your life tell us a great deal about the defense mechanisms you typically use.

In recent years, the media have focused attention on the so-called "personality disorders," raising public awareness of a type of psychological difficulty so profound that it *defines* an individual's personality, shaping his or her relationships in recognizable ways. Men and women who suffer from Narcissistic Personality Disorder[6] usually have an inflated sense of their own importance, lack empathy for others and react to criticism with anger or shame. Those who suffer from Borderline Personality Disorder are impulsive, emotionally volatile and have unstable relationships with other people.

This diagnostic labeling, based on the way emotional difficulties may define a personality, is a clinical, codified version of the everyday type of psychological summation we all employ: our language is full of expressions we use to sum up people whose personalities reflect characteristic ways of relating. Consider the statements below. These are expressions and ways of describing other people which most of us have relied upon at one time or another. Because these refer to character traits that tend to cause friction or difficulty in relationships, people often mean something critical or judgmental when they use them:

---

[5] *Ibid*, pp. 51-52.

[6] In the upcoming revision to the Diagnostic and Statistical Manual published by the American Psychiatric Association, this diagnostic label will apparently be eliminated.

A is such a control freak.

B always makes me feel like I have to rescue him.

C is easy to deal with as long as things go her way.

D is way too needy for me.

E is such a cold fish.

F gets so hysterical about everything.

Why is G always so uptight?

That H – what a hothead!

J is such a drama queen!

K thinks he's God's gift to women.

L is such a timid little mouse.

Why does M always make herself a doormat in her relationships?

These descriptions distill a particular trait or style of relating and use it to define our idea of someone's basic personality. Although less obvious, they also point to those areas where the person has the most difficulty: (1) coping with *need and dependency* for **A** through **D**; (2) managing intense and often painful *emotions* for **E** through **H**; and (3) issues of *self-esteem* in relation to others for **J** through **M**.

In Chapter Two, we'll examine each of these areas in detail, exploring what I refer to as life's *primary psychological concerns*. It is our relative difficulty in bearing with these challenges that for the most part determines which psychological defense mechanisms we use.

Each one of us develops his or her *individual* constellation of defenses to cope with *universal* emotions. Cultures may differ in the ways they condone or condemn certain feelings, thus shaping our personalities and the ways we ward off socially unacceptable emotions, but people everywhere struggle with the same basic challenges inherent in the human experience:

1. Needing or desiring contact with other people and depending upon them for what we need; bearing frustration, disappointment or helplessness in those relationships.

2. Coping with difficult, often painful emotions such as fear, anxiety, anger, hatred, envy and jealousy.

3. Feeling good about ourselves and confident of our personal worth in relation to others.

Different people find different issues to be more difficult; two people may struggle with the same emotional challenge and defend against it in entirely different ways. For all of us, the defense mechanisms we use will shape our personalities and profoundly affect our interpersonal relationships.

What About You?

At this point, you're probably wondering, "So what *are* these different psychological defense mechanisms?" Or even more likely: "What defenses do *I* use?" The remainder of this book will be devoted to explaining the typical defenses we all employ, with examples drawn from my practice as well as everyday experiences we can all recognize. To bring it home, this and each of the following chapters in the first two parts will include a set of questions/exercises that will help you see your own psychological defenses in action and understand why you're doing what you do.

Making Use of the Exercises in this Book

As a prelude to the first exercise, go back and take another look at personality descriptions **A** through **M** from the last section (p. 13). One or two of them might apply to you, possibly in a less extreme form.

Maybe somebody once hurt your feelings by describing you in just those terms: *Why do you have to get so hysterical about everything?* Or: *You're always so uptight! Can't you just relax?* If so, you might have felt self-protective—*defensive*, in the everyday sense of that word. When people tell us things about ourselves in critical language, or resort to character assassination by using words like *always* and *everything*, we naturally find it difficult to listen, however accurate their observations may be.

Even when a friend makes a concerned or loving observation about us, we may want to reject it. Sometimes, no matter how kindly put, such a remark will make us *defensive*. As you review those 12 personality descriptions from above, you may insist to yourself that none applies to you, not even in a less extreme form. Or you may think something like, *There might be some truth to that,* **but**…When you remember our basic definition of defense mechanisms—*lies we tell ourselves to ward off pain*—such a reaction might mean that one of your defense mechanisms is at work. The emphatic word *but* often indicates just that. We tend to become defensive when confronted with something painful.

Freud and the many psychodynamic therapists who have followed him refer to this phenomenon as *resistance.* You've probably heard that word before; it's not a difficult concept to grasp. If we originally warded off feelings or facts too painful to bear—that is, resorted to a defense mechanism—we will naturally *resist* anything that threatens to revive that pain. Sometimes we reject an idea simply because it doesn't ring true for us. On other occasions, though, we resist it because we find it threatening or painful. In that latter case, our resistance to the idea reveals the operation of one of our defense mechanisms.

In my psychotherapy practice, I witness my clients' resistance on a daily basis; without being too confrontational, I draw their attention to this resistance and gently encourage them to think about what it means. If you're not in some kind of therapy, you'll have to do the job of a psychotherapist for yourself as you work through this book, making note of your resistance when it arises. With patience but also with firmness, you'll have to ask yourself the hard questions:

Why do I keep coming back to this idea, over and over, insisting that it's not true?

What is it about the passage that irritates me so much?

Why haven't I picked up that defenses book since reading the bit that reminded me of... now what was it?

Why did I move on so quickly after reading that case study?

I suggest that, while reading this book, you keep a notebook or journal and track your reactions. Store it in a secure place and make sure no one else has access to it. You'll have a harder time recording those shameful or distressing observations if you're worried that someone might read them. Be as honest and non-judgmental as you can. Try to focus simply on *what is* – the ways you actually do feel, your unedited reactions – rather than how you think you *ought* to respond. Don't push yourself toward changing.

In regard to the end-of-chapter exercises: write down your answers, making note of any particularly strong or unusual reactions you may have. As you progress to later chapters, occasionally go back and revisit your earlier responses. You might find that your views and understanding will change over time. And if you don't want to do the exercises or answer the questions, make note of that, too. Resistance shows up in many different ways!

EXERCISES

As with all the exercises in this book, record your responses in your journal. You could do so in a narrative format or instead make brief notes in summary.

1. When you think about some of the people you know, do you believe there are things you can observe and identify about them that they don't see? Why do you think they don't recognize this aspect of themselves? In what way would it be painful for them to admit the truth?

2. At the beginning of the chapter, I gave a few examples of people "waking up" to an emotion they hadn't realized they were

feeling beforehand. Has that ever happened to you? What was the emotion you ultimately felt? Was it unpleasant or painful?

3. Has anyone ever told you something about yourself that deeply upset you, which made you "defensive" in the everyday sense of that word? Looking back on the experience now, is there any element of what the person said that might be true?

Now What?

The simple exercise above aims merely to get you thinking about the reality of defenses, in yourself as well as in other people, and to focus on the ways we all try to avoid painful truths. Tomorrow and during the days that follow, see if you can spot any "lies" that friends, colleagues or family members may be telling themselves in order to evade pain. Begin to ask yourself what unpleasant truths you, too, might not want to face.

TWO

Our Primary Psychological Concerns

To be is to be vulnerable.
– Norman O. Brown

Consider the following statements about our species:

1. Human beings are primates with a long helpless infancy and an even longer dependent childhood.

2. In order to survive in a dangerous world, we evolved a system of intense emotional responses that help us cope with crucial situations and react quickly to threatening stimuli.

3. Homo sapiens are social animals who, historically speaking, have always lived within packs or tribes that have a complex internal hierarchy; a psychological/emotional inter-connectedness between members binds the pack together and promotes survival of the species.

These features may sound like interesting anthropological facts without much impact upon you personally, or upon your daily concerns, but in truth, each one plays a profound role in our lives. They also affect each and every one of our relationships—between parent and child, among friends or colleagues, between lovers. And they lie at the heart of the individual search for a sense of personal meaning and self-worth.

From a developmental perspective, here are some of the ways that our evolutionary heritage shapes our personal life stories, the personalities we develop and the psychological issues that may trouble us.

1. *Because of our lengthy, vulnerable childhood—where for so many years we rely upon our parents to meet our needs and protect us from the dangers of the world—the issue of dependency lies at the core of the human experience. If our needs aren't met during infancy when we're utterly vulnerable and helpless, if our parents make us feel unsafe in the world from early on, it will shape our ability to trust and depend upon other people for the rest of our lives.*

Consider the case of Brian, one of my clients, whose father abandoned the family during Brian's infancy and whose mother subsequently went from one short-term relationship to another. As an adult, Brian was a loner who found it difficult to trust or depend upon anyone. When he married, he chose a woman he could easily control and secretly installed surveillance equipment in the house to monitor her movements.

Another client, Melissa, came from a similarly chaotic background; she became clingy and possessive in her friendships as well as her romantic relationships. From the moment she formed a new connection, she'd become preoccupied with the other person, worrying that he or she would drop her.

2. *Beginning at birth, babies have powerful feelings and fears about the world in which they live. A big part of their parents' job is to help them manage those feelings—to calm and make them feel safe, for example, or to soothe them when they hurt. If we grow up with caretakers who let us down, who don't provide the emotional support we need, we will always have a hard time managing our own feelings.*

I worked for a number of years with a young woman I'll call Sharon, who came to see me for help with an uncontrollable cycle of bingeing-and-purging. Her parents divorced early and her mother ran the lives of her children with military precision, shunning intense emotion or conflict of any kind, so much so that she lived in a state of denial that her second husband was molesting Sharon. As an adult, Sharon couldn't bear strong emotions and used food to anesthetize herself; vomiting served as an unconscious means to evacuate unbearable feelings and left her in a state of placid emptiness...for a time.

Another client, Aidan, who came from an extremely disturbed and emotionally volatile family, continually felt overwhelmed by his own feelings. Small problems at work became major crises; frustration often led to explosive outbursts with his co-workers. When he had to deal with conflict in his relationships, it would frequently end in an emotional meltdown.

> 3. *Each of us needs to feel that we matter and have a place in the world; we need a sense of internal worth and to feel that the other people in our lives (our "pack") value and respect us. When our early environment doesn't instill us with this sense of individual worth and value, we'll struggle with issues of shame and low self-esteem throughout our lives.*

Sam was the child of harsh and perfectionistic parents who made him feel that little he did measured up to their standards. He grew into a tall and extremely handsome man but couldn't shake the feeling that he was ugly. As an adult, though married and ostensibly heterosexual, he would occasionally visit gay bath houses when he felt especially low. He never engaged in sexual activity there, but thrived on the admiration and desire he could see in other men's eyes.

Jessica, another client, came from a large family with a history of drug abuse, mental illness and broken marriages. As Jessica grew up, her mother tended to idealize her—for her artistic talents and excellence in school—the one child who was not a "failure," but Jessica never felt any confidence in her own abilities. For as long as she could remember, she'd felt crippled by shame; as an adult, she couldn't fulfill her artistic promise, never had a relationship that didn't turn out to be emotionally abusive, always gave much more than she received and asked for very little in her friendships.

These three primary psychological concerns lie at the heart of the human experience. During the years I've practiced as a therapist, virtually every person who came to see me struggled with one of or more of them.

Some clients can't bear the dependent nature of intense personal relationships; like Brian, they're unable to get close, or like Melissa, get "too close."

In individual psychotherapy, my clients and I explore the psychological defenses they use to ward off the awareness of their own needs, in the process helping them to better tolerate those needs—a necessary step toward more fulfilling relationships. For readers who struggle with similar issues, this book will identify the defense mechanisms typically used to cope with unbearable neediness and offer guidance for how to disarm those defenses, at the same time teaching more effective ways to bear those needs.

Other clients find their emotional lives unmanageable. Either they shut down and develop ways to rid themselves of emotion, as Sharon did with her binge-eating, or they feel themselves to be at the mercy of their own emotions, constantly overwhelmed by feeling like Aidan.

In the context of the psychotherapy relationship, such clients come to recognize the defensive strategies they employ in order to manage emotion, along the way learning better ways to cope with their feelings. Parts II and III of this book guide the reader through a similar process.

Most clients battle for a sense of self-worth. Like Sam, many people crave intense admiration from others, or try to draw attention to themselves in order to escape from self-hatred or feelings of personal worthlessness. Some people are burdened by shame for life, like Jessica; they feel unworthy and lack the confidence to succeed in life or to have healthy relationships.

As a psychotherapist, a central focus of my work is the issue of shame—helping clients recognize the reasons they feel the way they do, narcissistic defenses they mobilize to ward off shame, or the perfectionistic, self-hating ways they "kill off" their shame-ridden, damaged selves. This book explores the characteristic defenses against shame and teaches a different way to recognize and cope with it.

*   *   *

One or more of the above descriptions might ring true for you.

Perhaps you can't form satisfying relationships that last, either because you have a hard time getting close, or because other people find you too possessive or "clingy." You might be someone who frequently over-reacts and feels bad about it later; or you're shut down and not aware of what you're really feeling. You may have suffered throughout your life from feelings of low self-esteem, even self-hatred.

In my experience, most people struggle with these issues in one way or another. They also ward off the pain involved using a variety of defense mechanisms, some more successfully than others. When their defense is relatively stable and effective, people rarely seek psychotherapy (or buy books like this one). They have achieved an emotional equilibrium that makes life bearable, even if they had to sacrifice some aspects of their emotional lives. Not every painful feeling must be acknowledged and felt. There are situations where psychological defense mechanisms *help us* manage the pain of life and therefore prove useful. Not everyone needs or wants psychotherapy.

It is usually when a defense mechanism doesn't work well enough, or makes our pain worse rather than better, that we seek professional help. Maybe it's why you decided to buy this book. There may be some compulsive behavior that's interfering with your life and relationships. Or a destructive pattern you don't understand and can't seem to break. You might react to other people in ways you're unable to control and which cause you a great deal of pain or humiliation. Perhaps your relationships feel mostly broken and unsuccessful.

These are signs that a psychological defense mechanism is no longer helping you, or is causing more pain than it was intended to cure. It means that you're struggling with one or more of the three areas of primary psychological concern: (1) bearing need and dependency as an inevitable part of relationships; (2) managing intense emotions; or (3) developing a sense of self-esteem (as opposed to a sense of shame and a feeling that you are damaged).

It also means you need to find more effective ways to cope, and the aim of Part III is to teach you how.

Theoretical Views on the Primary Psychological Concerns

[For those readers without much interest in theory or the history of these ideas, you can skip ahead to the Exercises without loss of continuity.]

Almost everyone knows that Sigmund Freud stressed the importance of the sexual instincts (libido) in human nature, shocking his contemporaries with theories about childhood sexuality in the oral and anal phases. In his *Three Essays on Sexuality* (1905), he made his first mention of the *source*, *aim* and *object* of an instinct, repeatedly returning to these concepts in later works: "We can distinguish an instinct's source, object and aim. Its source is a state of excitation in the body [and] its aim is the removal of that excitation..."[7]

Especially in his early works, Freud can sometimes sounds mechanistic, like a biologist speaking of a build-up in sexual tension and its subsequent release without any reference to human relationships. Implicit in all Freud's theories, however, is the idea that instincts are by nature *object-seeking*—that is, we humans have an inbuilt drive

---

[7](1933) *New Introductory Lectures on Psycho-Analysis,* S.E. **22**, p. 96.

to connect with *other humans*, not simply to find a convenient release for sexual tension. In the quote above, an instinct's third feature is its *object*; from the outset, psychoanalytic theory has used that unfortunate term to refer to people other than the individual in question (as in *object* versus *subject*).

This idea of a drive for connection with other humans lies at the heart of the Object Relations school of thought, developed by theorists such as Ronald Fairbairn, Melanie Klein, Donald Winnicott and Harry Guntrip during the 1940s and 1950s. Although Object Relations retains much of the language of Freudian libido theory, it largely shifts the emphasis from sex drive to the mother-infant feeding relationship. It focuses on early infantile dependency–the experience of need, longing and frustration. Today, most psychodynamic therapists use such a paradigm to understand their clients.

How did the client experience early childhood, when she was utterly helpless and dependent upon her parents, particularly her mother?

How did the parents' limitations and failures impact his development? Was his early experience of needing people unbearably frustrating?

How are their present-day relationships affected by those early experiences?

In other words, Object Relations Theory, as an expansion of Freudian thought, examines the first of our primary psychological concerns: the experience of need for and dependence upon other people.

Many subsequent theorists have expanded our understanding of the early mother-infant relationship, focusing on the mother's role in helping the undeveloped baby learn to manage its own emotional experience. Donald Winnicott's notion of the "holding environment," Heinz Kohut's focus on empathy, and W.R. Bion's view of the mother's role in "containing" her child's unbearable emotional experience–all three speak to the ways a mother helps her child to tolerate, understand and ultimately think about its emotional experience. These theorists address the second of our primary psychological concerns: how we learn to manage our feelings. Most psychodynamic therapists have been impacted by such theories:

Why does my client have such low tolerance for strong feeling? Was her mother emotionally unavailable? Or possibly the opposite, too chaotic and frightening?

In the context of our sessions, how can I help him to bear with that explosive rage and not be overwhelmed by it? The fact that his mother was so unstable and utterly unreliable must have been a factor.

Heinz Kohut not only wrote only about empathy and its role in object relations, but he expanded our understanding of an individual's experience of *self*—what it feels like to be who she is within herself, how she struggles with issues of identity, personal meaning and self-expression. More recently, Andrew Morrison has shed light on the role of profound shame in disorders of the self, including narcissism.[8] These theorists probe the third of our primary psychological concerns: our search for both an internal sense of personal worth and the conviction that we are valued by others. In thinking about a client, a psychodynamic psychotherapist might believe:

The violence and utter chaos of her early family life has left this woman burdened with a deep sense of shame about the ways in which she is "not normal."

His depressed and self-absorbed mother had no room for her baby, and almost no capacity to love or nurture him; as a result, he grew up with little sense of self, no feeling of his worth and value as a person.

The following exercise will help you take a deeper look at each of those primary psychological concerns in order to find out which one(s) poses the greatest difficulty for you.

---

[8]Andrew P. Morrison. *Shame: The Underside of Narcissism* (New York: Rutledge, 1997).

EXERCISE

The following statements are grouped into three clusters, with two subgroups for each cluster. Go through all the statements once or twice to determine which particular cluster speaks more to you than the others. Then go through that cluster again and decide which sub-group more accurately describes you. Write down those choices in your journal.

Make sure you're clear on which Group Number(s) you've chosen because I'll be referring to them throughout Part II.

Even if you're storing that journal safely, you might find yourself wondering what other people would think if they could see your choices, as if someone were standing behind you and looking over your shoulder. Try to put such thoughts aside; if they're particularly strong, write down exactly what you imagine those "other people" are thinking. Another obstacle will be your expectations for yourself and the "you" you'd like to be. As I'll discuss in the later chapters of this book, developing a kind of open-eyed honesty—neither too harsh nor too easy in its evaluations—is a necessary step in learning to disarm your defenses. Evaluate yourself as objectively as you can.

And don't read the discussion that follows the exercise until you've completed it!

Cluster A

Group 1

I don't trust other people to be there when I need them.

I keep getting involved with the same clingy-type.

Feeling too needy and dependent is a weakness.

I rarely overeat or drink too much and have a good handle on my appetites.

Sex doesn't matter as much to me as it does to other people.

If you want something done right, you should do it yourself

Group2

> When a problem comes up, I often fantasize that someone will "fix" it for me.
>
> I don't exactly binge but I wish I had more control over my eating.
>
> When I get romantically involved, it's all-consuming.
>
> Sometimes I feel way too needy.
>
> Now and then I end up having sex on a date even though I know it's a bad idea.
>
> Other people seem to matter more to me than I do to them.

Cluster B

Group 3

> Strong displays of emotion make me uneasy.
>
> I almost never cry, except once in a while during a sad movie.
>
> I rarely get angry and never lose my temper.
>
> I'm an extremely nice person.
>
> I often start on something new and quickly lose interest.
>
> I worry that something bad will happen if I'm not extremely careful.

Group 4

> I often overreact to situations and feel bad about it later.
>
> It's not unusual for me to feel emotionally overwhelmed.
>
> I wish I didn't have these mood swings.
>
> I often feel disorganized and out of control.
>
> I've lost my temper more times than I care to remember.
>
> I feel as if I'm sitting on a whole lot of intense feelings.

Cluster C

Group 5

> I probably spend too much time in front of the mirror.

A big part of my budget is for new clothes and taking care of my
appearance.

Other people often wish they had my looks/success/personality.

In terms of relationships, it's hard to find anyone who meets my
standards.

At parties, I love to be in the spotlight.

It's not unusual for me to feel impatient with or contemptuous
of other people.

Group 6

I often feel "beneath" my friends and acquaintances.

I tend to beat myself up over mistakes I make.

I often feel envious of other people and the lives they lead.

I worry that other people look down on me.

I have a really hard time with criticism and get very defensive.

I wish I were someone else.

As you went through the exercise, you might have noticed that
the statements for Cluster A have to do with issues of need, desire and
dependency. Cluster B focuses on powerful emotions and self-control,
while Cluster C concerns issues of self-esteem and how we view ourselves in relation to others.

Readers who relate most to **Group 1** statements have a hard time
acknowledging need and depending upon other people; their defenses
will be geared toward denying dependency and persuading themselves
that they don't feel desire or need.

People who identify strongly with **Group 2** statements instead
get "carried away" by their needs and desires; with characteristic defense
mechanisms, they attempt to master themselves by gaining control over
what they need.

Readers who gravitate toward **Group 3** statements likely feel
uncomfortable with intense emotions; their defense mechanisms will be

oriented toward avoiding situations that might give rise to strong feeling or toward reducing the impact of such feelings when they arise.

Those drawn to **Group 4** statements often feel overwhelmed by their feelings; their defense mechanisms aim to "get rid" of those feelings in various ways, or to find ways to hold onto one particular feeling versus another.

Individuals who are drawn to Cluster C statements, whether **Group 5** or **Group 6**, struggle with feelings of shame and low self-esteem. The defense mechanisms of those who identify with **Group 5** statements are meant to convince themselves and other people that the *exact opposite* is true.

People who identify with **Group 6** statements have defense mechanisms that have largely (but not entirely) failed them, although the desire to become another person entirely is, in itself, a type of defense mechanism. I'll have more to say about this issue in Chapter 11, *Defenses against Shame.*

Now What?

You may find that many of the statements from different clusters resonate and that you don't fall into one particular group. For example, both the Group 1 and Group 3 statements often speak to the same people. The point is not to pigeonhole yourself but rather to get a sense of *where your emotional challenges lie*, as a prelude to identifying the defense mechanisms you use to cope with them. On some level, to one degree or another, everyone struggles with all of these issues.

Pay attention to the way these issues come up in your daily life. Notice how you and other people respond to feeling needy or wanting something. It could be as simple a matter as asking someone to bring you a soda from the kitchen. Watch for different ways of coping with strong feeling, whether the people around you tend to blow up or shut down. Check your sense of self-esteem in relation to other people and ask yourself how you imagine they feel in relation to you.

Before continuing to the next chapter, be sure you're clear on which group(s) of statements from the Exercise best describe you. Memorize the number(s).

THREE

The Emotional Landscape

There is no coming to consciousness without pain.
– Carl Jung

In the last chapter, we looked at the three primary psychological concerns at the heart of the human experience—bearing neediness, tolerating intense feelings and developing a sense of personal worth and value. Although the second of those concerns focuses in particular on emotion, all three areas involve characteristic feelings that human beings everywhere feel, at one time or another. **Coping with our primary psychological concerns means facing and accepting a broad range of emotions**.

Having ordinary human needs means we long for contact with others; we crave physical closeness and intimacy, we wish for friends and desire sex. When we get what we need, we may feel happy and gratified; when we don't, it might make us feel sad, lonely or frustrated. And if we're unbearably frustrated, it might stir up anger, resentment or even hatred.

Developing a sense of personal worth involves feelings of pride, a sense of integrity and well-being that leads to contentment, with oneself and one's world. Strong self-esteem also links to happiness and fulfillment. The alternative, shame, is one of the most deeply painful feelings we know. It interferes with the experience of happiness and contentment. It darkens the entire emotional spectrum; it stops us from getting what we need.

Thus coping with our areas of primary concern inevitably stirs up intense feelings; navigating them well means learning to tolerate that intensity, both pleasurable and painful. It means accepting that the human condition involves a wide range of emotions we can't avoid.

"All I Want is to be Happy"

As a therapist, one of the first challenges I often confront with a new client concerns this very issue – the inevitability of certain painful feelings. Early in my own treatment, I said something to my therapist like, "I just want to be happy." I said this more than once, in various different ways. He often answered me with a question: "Are you interested in learning what you actually do feel, or only in feeling one particular way?" Over the years, I've heard my own clients make similar statements; I've usually responded in the same vein as my therapist did to me.

Everyone wants to be happy and feel love for others. It's understandable, and there's no shortage of professional advice about how to get there. Walk down the self-help aisle at Barnes & Noble and you'll find many books that map out the path to happiness, or teach you how to achieve unconditional love. Others offer guidance for *overcoming* one "negative" feeling or another. While I understand the longing for happiness, the desire to feel love and the wish to transcend difficult, painful feelings, this book proposes a different attitude toward our emotions.

Feelings are transient experiences; they come and go, and no one feels only one way at all times, of course. In that sense it's not possible to achieve "happiness," as if you could arrive at that state of being and stay there. Even if you're happily married with a career you love, death will come to someone you care about – your parents or other loved ones. Even if you achieve a fair measure of success and personal fulfillment, the economy may take a downturn, traffic on the interstate with still back up, salesclerks will be rude, flights will be canceled, things will go wrong and accidents will happen. Frustration, disappointment, anger, sadness and grief are all inescapable parts of the human experience. In the end, everyone has to confront the inevitability of his or her own death.

It's natural for us to try avoiding that pain whenever possible. We'll find a different route in order to avoid the Friday afternoon traffic jam on our commute home; we'll make sure not to shop at that store where the clerk snapped at us; we'll drop those acquaintances that routinely hurt our feelings. Much of the time, however, it's impossible to anticipate or avoid pain. In those cases, we need to bear with the pain, frustration or disappointment. Sometimes there's a lesson to be learned—*I'll never trust Holly again; she's let me down one time too many*—but often there's nothing to do but suffer through it until the feeling passes.

In my experience, a great many people have a difficult time *suffering* their experience, in the secondary sense of that word: *to put up with especially as inevitable or unavoidable.* They may want to get rid of their feelings (by using alcohol or illicit drugs), distract themselves, even deceive themselves as to the truth of what they feel—by resorting to the various defense mechanisms we'll discuss in Part II of this book.

Before we go on to learn about those defenses, we first need to discuss the human emotional landscape—the kinds of feelings that all of us feel and struggle with at one time or another as we navigate our primary psychological concerns. If we're fully alive to ourselves and our experience, we can't avoid those feelings. It is the most painful of these emotions that often cause us to resort to our defense mechanisms.

Aristotle's List of Emotions

Over the centuries, many theorists have attempted to put forth a definitive catalog of our emotions. Although he wrote more than 2,000 years ago, Aristotle sets forth the list that I find most useful for my purposes.

In Book Two of his *Rhetoric,* he tells us that our basic emotional makeup consists of seven opposing pairs:

Anger and Calmness

Hatred and Love

Fear and Confidence

Shame and Shamelessness

Gratitude and its Lack

Pity (or Empathy) and Indignation

Envy and Emulation

Because he's writing about *rhetoric,* or public discourse, Aristotle emphasizes the way emotions affect our judgment, and how a public speaker can arouse feelings in his audience in order to persuade; I'll be focusing instead on the way these emotions inevitably come up in the context of our relationships, with particular emphasis on the ones we find the most difficult to bear and which most often trigger a defense mechanism.

I group them in a slightly different way, in an order geared to address the primary psychological concerns and based on stages of emotional development we optimally pass through as we grow from infancy to adulthood. It doesn't include every emotion you'll ever feel; it's not exhaustive, but it does cover the major emotions we humans experience, highlighting the ones that cause us the most pain and difficulty.

Like most psychodynamic therapists, I think a lot about babies and their earliest experiences. The environment we meet when we emerge from the womb, how it helps or hinders us in coping with our primary psychological concerns, will play a major part in shaping the adult people we become. Some of the most painful emotions, ones which we may struggle with throughout our lives, are the first ones we feel.

Fear, Anger and Hatred

Listening to the screams of a newborn infant is a very uncomfortable experience. Those cries evoke all sorts of painful feelings in you, as the listener; if you tune into your own reactions, you get a sense of what the infant may be feeling. *Fear*, to begin with. The newborn's cry conveys its terror at the new and unpredictable experiences confronting it in life-outside-the-womb. Infants often sound *angry*, too—as if they *hate* the way they are feeling, or even feel persecuted by it.[9]

Perhaps the infant is hungry, cold, physically uncomfortable or just exhausted. Because such new and unfamiliar experiences are painful, they frighten the baby; it has no idea how long such experiences will last. Babies become angry if their discomfort goes on too long; they may feel persecuted by sensations they can't escape and even come to hate them. These, I believe, are our earliest reactions to unfamiliar or painful experiences; to varying degrees, they continue throughout our lives.

A great many adults are afraid of the new and unfamiliar experience. Such fear makes us risk-adverse, unwilling to give up the familiar for the unknown, to take a chance on a new job, new relationship, even a different haircut. Many people get stuck in rigid routines, afraid to break the pattern and do something unexpected; the reasons may be complicated, but anxiety about what they might feel if things were to change is usually one of them. A fear of unexpected, unpredictable emotions will often bring defense mechanisms into play so that we exclude those feelings from awareness before they can cause trouble.

And how many of us become grouchy when we're tired, hungry or in pain, snapping at those around us? "Don't take it out on me," people often say in response. Our grouchiness is an expression of anger, aroused by those unpleasant experiences, and we often direct it at people nearby, as if it were their fault. We may become angry when we feel ways that we don't like, and sometimes we will hate the people who we believe have made us feel that way. It's usually not fair: you aren't actually to blame for the way I feel right now, but that doesn't stop me from biting your head off, as if you were!

---

[9] In speaking of hatred at this early stage, I don't mean to suggest that an infant hates its mother; rather, *it hates its own emotional and physical experience of pain.*

Occasional fear, anger and even hatred are inevitable parts of the emotional landscape.

Calmness and Confidence

If the emotional environment supplies the infant with what it needs—that is, if a parent picks it up, feeds and comforts it, changes its diaper, etc.—the baby's fear will abate and it will *calm* down. Anger and hatred will fade as the discomfort goes away.

Hunger will eventually return, of course, as will fatigue and other kinds of physical discomfort, stirring anew the feelings of fear, anger and sometimes hatred. But with repeated experiences of returning to a state of calm when its parents provide what is needed, the baby gradually develops a sense of safety in its world. Memories of being fed and comforted will accumulate; over time, the baby comes to feel *confident* that its caretakers will once again appear and offer help the next time pain arises.

Such consistent experiences of reliable care, of being returned again and again to a state of calm, not only make the baby feel confident in its caretakers, but form the basis for feelings of *self-confidence*, as well. Accumulated memories of surviving those painful moments make the baby feel confident that it will be able to survive the next time those feelings come up. The ability to weather one's emotional storms, to get through one's own experience and to survive, is the foundation of what we will later call self-esteem or self-confidence.

Think of a person you consider emotionally steady and fairly self-confident—neither arrogant nor detached, and not necessarily special in any particular way—just an ordinary, well-balanced, reasonably contented person. Chances are, that person grew up in a family that provided the kind of emotional environment I've described. It wasn't perfect…just "good enough," in Winnicott's terms. When the environment is more or less reliable, good enough at responding to our needs, it's like food for the psyche and we can grow into "normal" adults.

> *A good enough environment leads to self-confidence and the ability to weather our emotional storms.*

Shame

What happens when the parents do *not* calm the infant, don't give what is needed or even worse, reject the baby and respond with feelings of hostility? Many parents are emotionally limited themselves, unable to bear the deprivations and challenges of parenting; they may hate those ways that their baby makes them feel and then turn away. Too many parents are so absorbed in their own needs and personal struggles that they have little room left over for anyone else. Some unfortunate infants are born to parents who suffer from mental illness, are mired in depression, crippled by anxiety, or have a weak sense of themselves and their own boundaries.

What happens to babies who grow up in such an environment?

Instead of feeling safe in its world, confident that the food and emotional support it needs in order to thrive will be forthcoming, the baby's fear, anger and hatred become *unbearable*; because it has no ability to tolerate this excruciating experience, it can only *ward off* the awareness of it. Instead of learning to tolerate and understand its experience, the baby tries to *get rid of* it, or the awareness of it, relying on psychological defense mechanisms to protect itself.

Babies who come from such families never develop that fundamental sense of trust and safety in their world; they may be plagued by anxiety about what might happen. And instead of developing the *self-confidence* that goes along with trust, they may instead feel a deep sense of *shame*. This type of shame differs from later forms of shame which may result from *shaming messages* given by important figures in our lives.[10] It differs from the kind of shame we sometimes feel for violating

---

[10] John Bradshaw. *Healing the Shame that Binds You.* (Deerfield Beach, Florida: HCI, 1987).

acceptable codes of social behavior. The shame resulting from that pervasive experience of being let down by our parents afflicts us at the core of our being; it gives rise to a feeling that we are somehow different from other people, defective or even deformed. I'll discuss this type of shame in greater detail in Chapter Eleven.

You may have a friend who struggles with this type of shame – a talented person like my client Jessica described in the last chapter, who never seems able to fulfill her potential, who always gives far more than she receives, and goes from one abusive relationship to another. Or like Sam, my client who exhibited himself at bath houses because he felt so desperate to be admired and desired.

Shame is the crippling legacy of an impoverished childhood, one of the most powerful and least understood emotions that drive us to rely excessively on our defense mechanisms.

Envy and Jealousy[11]

Those of us who grow up burdened with shame and the sense of being damaged usually struggle with powerful feelings of envy and jealousy, as well. Being in the presence of people who have succeeded in life and achieved their goals, with a level of financial success beyond our own, often stirs up so much shame and a feeling of our own "inferiority" that we hate them for it. The idea that others possess something – a personal quality, a relationship or even a material possession – that we believe we'll never "own" ourselves might makes us want to belittle them, mock their achievements and cut them "down to size."

Even people who don't suffer from this type of shame may now and then feel envious. To some degree, envy is a normal experience; it

---

[11] I use the word *envy* to mean a painful or resentful awareness of an advantage enjoyed by another person joined with a desire to possess the same advantage, and *jealousy* to refer to the feelings that come up in relationships when there are issues of rivalry or unfaithfulness. In other words, envy involves two people *(you have something that I want)* and jealousy involves three *(I am threatened by your relationship with a third party)*.

teaches us what we want and may motivate us to work for it. Envy might be a slightly painful awareness that another person has something we wish we had for ourselves, but it doesn't always make us hate the other person or want to tear him or her down. When infused with shame, envy becomes unbearable and highly destructive: to find relief, we may want to annihilate the object of our envy.

Likewise, jealousy is a fairly common experience, a part of many relationships. Most of us have felt jealous on one occasion or another but it wasn't necessarily a major issue. If we care deeply for someone, we may sometimes feel left out when that person spends a lot of time with another close friend, a former life partner or a group we don't belong to, but it doesn't threaten us deeply. When we *do* feel deeply threatened, or find the experience of jealousy excruciating, it might be that there's a very good reason (our partner is having an affair, for example), or it may be a result of underlying shame, that sense of personal defect or unworthiness that results from early failures in our upbringing.

People with parents who consistently let them down emotionally and who failed to provide what was needed rarely feel safe in their adult relationships. What might be a minor, passing feeling of jealousy for one person will be unbearable for another. And if we struggle with deep shame, jealousy will be even more difficult because we doubt that we are loved; we fear that our damage and our defects make us *unlovable*. Jealousy becomes toxic because we fear that it's only a matter of time before our inner "truth" is revealed and we are rejected.

Envy and jealousy are normal emotions; when coupled with shame, they become unbearable.

Love, Gratitude and the Ability to Empathize

When things go well enough in our upbringing, when our caretakers make us feel safe and loved, and therefore self-confident, we also feel grateful to them for what they have given us. We develop a capacity for love. Having caretakers able to empathize with and respond appropriately to our needs and emotions enables us to do the same for others. If you get enough of what you need, you will feel grateful; if people around you understand your feelings and help you bear with them, then in later life, you'll be able to do the same for others.

Because empathy means imagining yourself in the shoes of another person, emotionally speaking–entering into that person's emotional experience–you have to be able to tolerate those emotions in order to empathize. When we don't get enough of what we need, when those people we depend upon are unable to empathize with our feelings, we may develop a very limited ability to empathize with the feelings of others as a result. Our capacity to feel genuine love for other people may be profoundly restricted. We may become preoccupied and overly self-involved–"narcissistic," in the sense that the word is commonly used today.

Or we may develop an over-active kind of empathy, where we become *too* focused on the needs of other people. In families where the parents had little to offer on an emotional level (were undeveloped and terribly needy themselves) children may grow up feeling that they can only get what they need for themselves by tending to the needs of others first. They may appear selfless in their devotion, but this type of empathy is less about other people than it seems; it's more about fulfilling some ideal self-image to combat shame, more about an unmet need than true generosity.

The capacity to feel gratitude, love and to empathize with the feelings of others results from a good-enough environment; self-absorption or a false kind of selflessness may result from too much deprivation.

*　　　*　　　*

This outline of optimal development and what can go wrong condenses years of my clinical experience, education and training; I wouldn't be surprised if you're feeling that it's an awful lot to take in. Don't worry. We'll revisit these ideas in chapters to follow; it might be a good idea to come back to this chapter and read it again later.

The central point of this discussion is that certain emotions, many of them painful, are inherent in the human experience and can't be entirely avoided. At different times, nearly all of us will confront these emotions. The following exercise should help you identify those feelings within your own experience.

EXERCISE

Try to recall a moment when you felt each of the following emotions. In your journal, write a description of that moment, with as much detail about the feeling as possible. If several experiences come to mind, focus on the more painful or difficult one. Remembering that emotion might include ways your body felt, fantasies it stirred up, judgments you made about yourself for feeling that way and, if you expressed it, how other people reacted to you. Probe deeply into the feeling and write everything down.

The list focuses on "negative" or painful feelings because these are the ones we usually don't want to feel and cause us the most trouble.

Highly agitated and full of apprehension

Agonizingly alone

Sexually frustrated

Almost unbearably needy

Powerfully angry

Sad, with a deep sense of loss

Full of hatred

Ashamed or humiliated

Painfully envious

Intensely jealous

If you can't think of a single instance to illustrate one of those feelings, make special note of it: that might indicate a defense mechanism at work (that is, you might have excluded it from awareness). As you write, make special note if you find yourself justifying the way you felt or blaming someone else for it; you might find that emotion particularly unacceptable within yourself.

*   *   *

After finishing this exercise with its emphasis on painful emotions, you may naturally feel exhausted. We don't normally spend so much time dredging up memories we'd prefer to forget…this might be a good time to take a break before reading on.

Now What?

Having completed the first three sets of exercises, you should have some basic sense of those primary psychological concerns that challenge you the most powerfully:

    a. In terms of basic human needs, you may be overly self-reliant or too dependent upon others.

    b. When it comes to emotion, you might feel too much or too little.

    c. You could be immobilized by shame on the one hand or continually running from it on the other.

The final exercise in this section should have helped you explore the most difficult of the human emotions as they arise in connection with our primary psychological concerns, possibly offering clues as to the ones that give you the most trouble.

With this knowledge, you're ready to learn about the individual defense mechanisms, how they work and which ones you may be using—the subject matter of Part II.

To Bear in Mind

Because of the specific, almost mechanistic nature of the concept, whenever we discuss psychological defenses, it's easy to believe that we're talking about isolated and precisely defined mental processes. In Part II,

I'll be discussing the defense mechanisms one by one in order to familiarize you with their features, but bear in mind that the separately-named psychological defenses are not in reality as discrete as those labels make them seem and can often be conceptualized in entirely different ways.

In the same vein, try to resist the current cultural trend toward applying diagnostic labels to everyone. These days, you so often hear that someone suffers from Bipolar Disorder, ADHD, PTSD, Narcissistic Personality Disorder or Borderline Personality Disorder, Seasonal Affective Disorder, and on and on. While there's a sort of comfort to be found in labels, as if we then know something truly important about ourselves or another person, in fact these artificially discrete categories mask the vast diversity of human experience. People aren't categories and no one fits neatly into any one of them.

I'm often told by prospective clients that they have been diagnosed with this or that disorder, as if they're telling me something crucial about themselves, but they begin treatment with no deeper insight than anyone else. From reading other books or listening to the media, you may have come to believe that you suffer from an identifiable, well-known disorder. Try to put that idea aside for the time being. Think about your unique background and personality rather than wedging yourself into a diagnostic category. Try to understand your own defensive maneuvers—what you do to evade the awareness of pain and why—instead of wondering which diagnostic label captures you best.

In other words, think more about *unbearable pain* than a specific mental process or diagnostic label. Focus more on what you might be avoiding and why you find it so painful, rather than worrying too much about which specific defense mechanism you employ or the DSM-IV category that describes you best.

All defense mechanisms, however we may conceptualize them, represent our efforts to evade, disguise or get rid of something inside that we find unacceptable or unbearably painful.

On to Part II.

PART II

Identifying Your Psychological Defenses

FOUR

Repression and Denial

Listen to you, you're so repressed.
– Clerks, 1994

Repression

When a low-budget indie film about two convenience store clerks incorporates a psychoanalytic concept into its dialog, we know that the concept has entered the cultural mainstream. Search the term "so repressed" on the Internet and you'll find it applied to Americans, Western women, Christians, the Japanese, the Irish, and so on. The concept of sexual repression is familiar to most of us and a recurring theme of Hollywood films, from *Splendor in the Grass* (1961) to *American Beauty* (1999).

Most people think about repression exclusively in connection with sexual issues, largely due to the importance of sexuality in Freudian thought and the way it was expressed in the 20th century assault on long-standing sexual taboos. While *repressed memory syndrome* can (hypothetically) develop as a result of various types of trauma, in the public mind it is most commonly associated with childhood sexual abuse. Ask anyone what *repression* means and the answer will most likely refer to sex.

Repression addresses a much larger range of experience, however; almost any unacceptable or painful feeling might be repressed from awareness, be it anger, guilt or grief. Repression was the first of the defense mechanisms to be identified by Sigmund Freud; early in his career, as he moved away from the use of hypnosis, he discovered that there was a psychic force that prevented a person from becoming aware of unacceptable impulses or ideas; it operated by *pushing them out of consciousness*.

In his paper on *Repression*, Freud describes the concept in simple terms: *"the essence of repression lies simply in turning something away, and keeping it at a distance, from the conscious."*[12] That "something" could be an unacceptable emotion or urge; it might be a perception about reality you'd rather not acknowledge. While Freud largely thought of the motive for repression as *evading conflict* – between our sexual urges and morality, for example – I find it more useful to remember Donald Meltzer's formulation (Chapter One), that all defenses (including repression) are essentially *lies we tell ourselves to evade pain*.

So when we repress something (*i.e.*, keep it at a distance from consciousness), it's because we're trying to avoid pain of one kind or another.

In the early years, Freud used the words "defense" and "repression" almost interchangeably. Sometimes he talks about repression as a distinct defense mechanism; at others, it seems to be a fundamental principle underlying *all* defense mechanisms: anything that has entered the realm of the unconscious must have been *repressed* from awareness. The other subject of this chapter – denial – is one of the primary defense mechanisms in its own right, but it also depends upon the work of repression.

Freud made clear that repression isn't something that happens just once; it's a process that requires a continual expenditure of mental energy to keep the repressed from returning to consciousness. In other words, we tend to develop ongoing strategies that are designed

---

[12]Sigmund Freud, *S.E.* **14**, p 147.

to keep the repressed feelings from breaking free of their dungeon. Learning to recognize the signs of that extra mental effort to keep something repressed is one of the ways we can identify when a defense mechanism is at work; I'll discuss this subject at greater length as we go along, especially in Part III.

Anyone who practices or has been in psychodynamic therapy most likely regards repression as an accepted fact of life, but there are many scientists and mental health professionals in other disciplines who will dispute its existence. Most self-help books make no reference to repression or to the unconscious. In those works, psychological growth seems to be mostly about un-learning maladaptive behaviors and thought patterns, mastering new cognitive-behavioral techniques and repeating affirmations.

In my view, if you don't understand how repression operates, real growth is nearly impossible since you're unlikely to come into contact with that pain you're warding off. Even if you're able to overcome some kind of maladaptive behavior or thought pattern, you're likely to develop another equally maladaptive strategy to keep the repressed at bay. Freud always insisted that unconscious material is "indestructible." Just because you're not consciously aware of how much anger you feel toward your father, that doesn't mean the anger has disappeared. It will inevitably continue to make its presence known in covert ways— humorous little digs, for instance, or sarcasm.

Unconscious Hostility and Passive-Aggressive Behavior

One of my clients, Olivia, came across as an exceptionally nice person. Impeccably dressed, meticulously polite, scrupulously thoughtful. She entered therapy for help with her pervasive feelings of anxiety. She had an apparently successful marriage, though the longer we worked together, the clearer became the emotional distance between Olivia and her husband Dan. Whatever complaints Dan had about his wife, he gave voice to only one of them, and frequently: that she had "butter fingers" and was always breaking things.

As our work eventually revealed, Olivia was sitting on a lot of unconscious rage. Much of that rage was the lasting residue of childhood – her super-authoritarian father, a retired military officer, allowed no dissent or expression of anger, and her alcoholic mother provided no emotional refuge. In her marriage, Olivia unconsciously felt a great deal of anger toward her husband (with and without reason), but because her family of origin had never helped her learn how to tolerate those feelings, she'd repressed her awareness of them. With time, we came to understand that "breaking things" was an unconscious expression of violent rage, a rage she found unacceptable and which she had to learn, little by little, how to tolerate.

Many people who repress hostility express it covertly and indirectly, in ways they usually don't recognize. *Passive-aggressive behavior* captures this dynamic – not in the clinical, diagnostic sense of that term but the everyday one we all understand. Instead of directly voicing anger or behaving aggressively, we might drag our feet about doing something important, complain and stubbornly resist cooperation, or simply "forget" to do it. As hard as it may be for others to believe – say, the spouse of such a passive-aggressor – many of these people are completely unaware of feeling angry. They've repressed awareness of their own hostility, which then finds covert expression in these alternative ways.

Repression and Resistance

Freud came to an understanding of repression through his clinical experience with *resistance* (Chapter Two, pp. 15-16). In the very early days, when he believed that recovering traumatic memories alone would be curative, he found that his patients didn't *want* to recover those memories, opposing his efforts to bring them to light. He decided that there must be some psychic force keeping the traumatic memory from entering consciousness. His clients' *resistance* to remembering something traumatic pointed to *repression* of their pain.

My own day-to-day encounters with resistance in my clients show me repression at work. Now and then I'll identify something clearly for my clients—some pain they're not facing, some level of shame they can't bear to feel—and when I try to help them to look at it, as empathically and sensitively as I can, they'll often insist that they do *not* feel that way; or they'll appear to agree with me and then change the subject. Sometimes they'll tell me that I'm just plain wrong (and of course, on occasion, I am!).

In more serious cases, they'll quit treatment if I get too close to the repressed material. I had a fairly typical experience with one new client, a woman whose childhood had been marked by psychological and sexual abuse, obviously in excruciating emotional pain. As she talked in session, she communicated that pain to me on a non-verbal level while she herself didn't seem aware of feeling it; when I tried on several occasions to draw her attention to that pain, reminding her of all the very good reasons she had for suffering, she half-heartedly agreed.

In subsequent weeks, she began to have scheduling conflicts, telling me she couldn't make our next session because she had a conference the next day and didn't want to be "distracted." After three more sessions, she decided not to come back. There are other possible explanations, of course. When someone terminates without an explanation, you never really know. But to me, the experience spoke to the enduring power of repression, and the resistance so often aroused in clients when I try to challenge it.

You might be feeling some resistance yourself right about now. In your thoughts, you might dispute whether repression really exists, or whether it's as important as I make it out to be. Maybe you believe that my former client made a wise choice when she decided to stop treatment with me. You, too, might like to "quit" by putting this book down instead of continuing to read.

Keep an open mind and read the next section anyway.

Denial

Like repression, the concept of denial has entered the mainstream. Almost everyone understands what it means if someone is "in denial." The term regularly shows up in TV shows and Hollywood films, the Pet Shop Boys wrote a song with that title, and we even make bad puns based on its similarity to the name of the Nile River. The term is so ubiquitous now that it makes the concept seem trivial, even irksome, but denial is a powerful force in the human psyche.

Virtually all psychotherapists recognize its existence, whether or not they regard it as clinically significant. With the popularization of her Five Stages of Grief, Elisabeth Kubler-Ross raised the public profile of denial (the first of those stages), and the prevalence of 12-step programs has also promoted awareness of the concept: a basic step in addressing addiction is to admit that you are an addict, rather than remain in denial about it.

"You're in denial" is something most people have said or heard at one point or another in their lifetimes. The expression generally refers to the denial of a *fact*: "You're in denial—Jane's obviously going to get the promotion, not you." Or: "He is never going to leave his wife—you're in denial." The concept is a simple one. An unacceptable fact exists, one that conflicts with our wishes or beliefs, and so we *deny* that it is true.

We may also deny a feeling, especially if we've received cultural or parental messages that tell us such a feeling is unacceptable. As a result of internalizing those messages, we may hide the existence of those feelings even from ourselves. "I do *not* feel angry because you forgot my birthday...again." Or: "No, I don't envy Emily. What's to envy?" When I first tried to make my client Olivia (pp. 51-52) aware of her unconscious anger, she told me I was wrong and remained in denial about it for some time.

In classical Freudian theory, it is the existence of a *conflict* that motivates denial (and other defenses): a fact conflicts with our wishes, or a feeling conflicts with our values so we deny it. I have a close friend who, during his late teens and early 20s, would often think to himself that turning out to be gay "was about the last thing" that would ever happen to him. He was in denial about his sexuality because it conflicted with his religious upbringing and all the negative societal messages about homosexuality he'd received during his childhood.

While the role of conflict in stimulating a psychological defense is certainly important, I believe pain plays the more important part. In the preceding example, the idea that he might be gay *pained* my friend; the conflict between his sexual identity and religious values *caused him pain.* For Olivia (as for everyone), being angry was a *painful* experience. The conflict between her own anger and those inherited family values that regarded such feelings as "bad" *caused her pain.*

Denial of Awareness

Whenever we employ denial, whether of a feeling or a fact, we are denying *our own awareness.* In other words, by using this particular defense mechanism, we refuse to recognize what we actually know on some level to be true, thus splitting our awareness and negating a part of it. Putting it that way makes it sounds like a conscious decision; on the contrary, all defense mechanisms occur unconsciously, outside of our awareness— if we knew we were doing it, the defense wouldn't work!

Here's another popular example: In the 1986 movie *Heartburn*, Rachel Samstat goes to her hairdresser one day; in listening to a story about another woman who didn't recognize the telltale signs that her husband was having an affair, Rachel gasps with a sudden horrified realization: the awareness had been growing in her that husband Mark was being unfaithful but she'd been insisting to herself and to other people that her marriage was a happy one. When she heard the hairdresser's story, the defense broke down and the painful truth she'd tried to avoid burst into consciousness.

Denial in Psychotherapy and in Everyday Life

Psychotherapists deal with denial in a variety of ways. Cognitive-behaviorists would avoid confronting the denial directly, instead teaching more effective behaviors for coping. Someone trained in psychodynamic psychotherapy might address it head on then watch the ways the client will defend against awareness. For instance, I might tell a client, "Contrary to what you keep saying about 'acceptance' and coming to terms with your mother's death, I think you can't bear how much you still miss her."

As I mentioned earlier in this chapter (pp. 50-51), repression or denial is not a one-time event; because the repressed or denied emotion always "wants" to escape, it's an unstable condition that requires continual effort to maintain. One typical sort of effort involves the repeating of the opposite, as in the example above: the client who keeps insisting she has come to terms with her mother's death when she really hasn't. This repetition may occur only in our thoughts—as it did with my friend, who kept telling himself he wasn't gay—or aloud, to other people, as Rachel Samstat does in *Heartburn*, frequently talking about how happy her marriage is. More than 400 years ago, Shakespeare neatly captured this dynamic and we echo his words to this day: "The lady doth protest too much, methinks" (*Hamlet*, III, ii).

Like other defenses, denial has its normal and useful functions. For instance, many of us deny that we are, in fact, actually going to die. If I'm honest with myself, I know that I don't really believe it—at least not all the time. If I did, I might have a hard time going on with my life and pursuing my goals. *What's the point of going to the gym today if my body will eventually fall apart and I'll die?* Sometimes, the temporary use of denial helps us cope with unbearable loss: we might deny that we feel profound grief because to confront the full force of our pain, all at once, might overwhelm us. We may need to let in the awareness of our loss little by little, over time.

What to Look For

Each of the chapters in Part II will include a discussion of the typical ways that the particular defense mechanisms may be used to cope with our primary psychological concerns: (a) need and dependency, (b) strong emotions and (c) self-esteem. After an overview of each defense, I'll explain how it shows up in those areas – how repressing the awareness of need and dependency might affect a person's character, or the things people say and do when they're in denial about their own anger. **Each chapter in Part II will follow the same format**. Using what you learned in Part I about your own areas of concern, you can then begin to look at your behavior, thoughts and feelings for signs that the defense mechanisms discussed in each chapter are at work.

Nobody uses every one of these defenses. In the chapter sections entitled *What to Look For*, I'll be linking each defense mechanism to outward signs and inner thought processes that will help you decide whether you might be relying on it and, in particular, how your reliance upon a defense mechanism may be affecting your relationships. I'll also discuss how you might recognize it at work in other people.

In the process, I'll be referring to the exercise from Chapter Two and the six groups of statements (pp. 27-29) designed to help you identify your own areas of concern. If it's not entirely clear which of these statement groups speaks most powerfully to you, I suggest you go back and review them now, and possibly again as we proceed to the other defense mechanisms.

One thing to bear in mind: if you feel that many of these descriptions apply to you, don't assume it means that you're deeply troubled or have a major problem with these issues. Each and every one of us relies upon defense mechanisms to get through life, and doing so is not a form of mental illness—it's *normal*. Only when we lean too heavily on defense mechanisms does it become a problem; only when using a psychological defense also hurts us in other important ways do we need to be concerned.

Need and Dependency

Many of us have a hard time bearing our needs and the fact that we, as human beings, must depend upon other people to meet those needs; often it's because our earliest experience of dependency was traumatic or grossly unreliable. As a result, we may *repress* the awareness of our needs, becoming highly independent and self-sufficient. We may *deny* that we feel certain needs or desires.

In many families, expressing needs is discouraged and self-reliance prized. As a result, members of those families learn to deny their needs and often become highly driven. On the one hand, an ability to repress the awareness of need helps people to pursue long-term goals that involve a lot of deprivation; extreme repression, on the other hand, can debilitate us if we deprive ourselves entirely of what we need. Denial of our need for and dependence upon other people may lead us to undervalue them, thereby damaging our relationships.

If you related most to the statements in **Group 1** from Chapter Three, you may rely upon repression to ward off the awareness of your own needs. If friends and family lean on you heavily to satisfy their own emotional or financial needs, and you never turn to others in the same way, you may be *in denial* about your own neediness. If you develop relationships with people who always seem to need you more than you need them, pay attention, especially if you feel disapproving or judgmental about people who need "too much."

As discussed above, repressed or denied needs don't entirely disappear, only our *awareness of them* has gone away; those unconscious needs will continue to express themselves in hidden ways. The workaholic with no time for relationships may begin to develop physical symptoms that require medical attention. Men and women who repress the awareness of their need for other people often turn to food, alcohol or drugs instead. One dynamic you often see in the addictive personality is the preference for a *substance*, something one can buy and theoretically control, rather than unreliable human contact.

If you have food or substance-related issues, you may be repressing or denying a different need, one connected to other people. If you feel little or no interest in sex, you almost certainly have repressed your desire. Likewise if you're preoccupied with pornography, especially when you have a romantic partner or spouse, you may be denying your need for and dependence upon another person to gratify your sexual needs – you can do it alone! If you have a hard time reaching out to people, it may be that you find your own neediness unacceptable. People who tell themselves they don't feel much need for friends, intimate relationships or sex are in denial.

Emotions

If you rely upon repression or denial to cope with intense feelings, you may have excluded those feelings from awareness and see yourself as a very calm, unflappable sort of person. Maybe you're always on an "even keel," with no horrible lows but without any wonderful highs either. People who repress their feelings tend to repress the entire spectrum of emotions, not just one or two of them.

If your life seems "flat" or you're often bored (that is, if you identified most with the statements in **Group 3**), repression may be at work. If your approach to life is highly logical, with little room for emotion, ask yourself where all your feelings have gone. Because emotion is the lifeblood of all interpersonal relationships, you may find yourself isolated, feeling out of touch with the people you know, whether they are friends, colleagues or romantic partners.

One of the most common feelings that people deny is anger. As discussed in Chapter Three, frustration, anger, rage and sometimes hatred are inevitable parts of the human emotional landscape and come up in all of our relationships at one time or another. If you *never* get angry, you may be in denial about it, especially if there are instances where you can objectively see legitimate grounds for anger. If there's a situation you know you ought to deal with but consistently avoid – maybe the way someone took advantage of you or let you down – it might be because you're afraid of your own anger and remain in denial of it.

In my experience, most families discourage the expression of anger. It can be a very destructive emotion, especially when it shows up in violent ways, but it also has value when we have good reason to feel angry – if we've been treated unjustly by a friend or co-worker, for example, or if someone deliberately tried to hurt us. Anger can motivate us to remove ourselves from destructive relationships and make needed changes in our lives. Anger helps us to fight injustice, whether at home, in the workplace or within the larger social arena.

Another emotion that people tend to repress is deep grief or sadness over loss. As a culture, we discourage lengthy grieving; many people consider tears a sign of weakness. If you're the sort of person who moves on quickly after a loss – the end of a relationship, say, or the loss of a friend – you may be repressing grief and sadness. If you're the sort of person who tells others that "there's no point in crying over spilt milk," you may tend to deny your own feelings of loss.

Self-Esteem

The experience of being emotionally damaged in some funda-mental way, of feeling a basic sense of shame about who we are, may be so painful that we repress or deny awareness of it. We may instead focus on making ourselves and our lives appear as if everything is "normal" or even superior as a kind of substitute for authentic self-esteem. If you find yourself preoccupied with appearances, wanting to make sure that other people perceive you as doing "just fine," or perhaps that you've got it all together – and if you identified most with the statements in **Group 5** – you may be repressing the awareness of shame.

People who deny their own feelings of damage or defect often develop conscious feelings of superiority, flaunting that superiority and demanding admiration. They may feel contempt for other people, viewed as beneath them; as a result, they have a hard time sustaining close contact with anyone. Because they've repressed their shame and feel threatened by anything that might make them feel ashamed, they also find it difficult to accept responsibility for mistakes they make, blaming others instead. Frequent blaming causes intense friction in relationships and may make the blamed person want to retreat from close contact. As a result, the blamer's friends, colleagues or loved ones may keep their emotional distance.

Each of these features – narcissism, contempt and blame – is a psychological defense in its own right, and I'll discuss them in detail in Chapter Eleven, *Defenses against Shame*.

EXERCISES

If you identified most strongly with statements from **Groups 2, 4** or **6**, repression and denial are not likely among your strongest defense mechanisms; as a result, this exercise may not engage you as fully as some of the ones to follow. Do your best with it anyway as it will acquaint you with the approach to be followed in subsequent chapters.

1. To help identify whether repression and denial play an outsized part in your psyche, see how many of these statements apply to you:

   • I experienced a major loss (say, the end of a friendship or romantic relationship) and felt little or nothing about it.

- I received a major insult or offense and didn't respond emotionally.

- When I finally achieved my goal, it didn't satisfy me as much as I expected.

- It seems that most other people tend to respond more intensely to life events than I do.

People with an especially intense fear of strong feelings may be *in denial* about one particular feeling or another, but they tend to *repress* the entire spectrum of their emotions. If you sometimes feel as if you aren't living your life to the fullest, with little emotional engagement in your career and relationships, intense repression is likely at work.

2. If you identified with the statements in Exercise 1 above: engage in some activity completely alien to your usual routine and with which you're unfamiliar. It could mean going to a new club to hear music you don't normally listen to. It could mean roller-blading. Or maybe you could drive to a part of town you don't know and walk along streets you've never seen before. (Make sure you're not in any danger, of course.) Talk to someone you don't know.

- Did you feel any internal resistance to stepping out of your routine?

- What feelings did the experience stir up?

- Did you notice yourself trying to put an end to or curtail those feelings? How?

- Did you find the experience in any way painful?

People who rely heavily on repression and denial to fend off strong feeling often organize their lives in ways to avoid situations that might stir it up, particularly by falling into narrow routine. In challenging yourself to confront new experience, you may recognize your resistance at work.

3. Review your past relationships–romantic, work and friend-ship–to see if there's a pattern of other people relying more on you than vice versa. If so, then you may be in denial about your own needs.

4. If you identified with Exercise 3, try turning to a friend, col-league or family member and asking for assistance. It could be something small, but when you ask, be sure to use the words "I need your help." You may have to fight your own resistance and all the excuses you'll invent for not asking. Observe your-self carefully at the moment of requesting help to see how you feel. The more discomfort you experience, the more likely it is that you're repressing your needs in general.

5. As part of the exercise in Chapter Three, I asked you to think about an instance where you felt ashamed or humiliated. Were you able to think of one? If you couldn't come up with a single instance, that likely indicates powerful repression at work since everyone feels ashamed at some point.

6. Take a good hard look at your behavior and what people have said about you:

   • Do you often find yourself becoming hot and highly defensive when a friend, colleague or family member finds fault with you?

   • Has anyone ever told you that you refuse to accept responsibil-ity for your mistakes and tend to blame others when something goes wrong?

   • Do your friends and family say, "You can't take criticism"?

   • Do you sometimes feel superior to and scornful of other peo-ple, especially those who seem to have emotional difficulties?

If you answered "yes" to any of these questions, it's likely that you struggle with underlying issues of shame but have repressed your awareness of it.

Now What?

These simple exercises should have helped you begin to recognize the role of repression and denial in your life. Everyone relies upon repression and denial to some degree; if you rely excessively upon it, you may find your emotional life constricted and have a difficult time developing relationships of any depth. Doing these exercises, you may have caught a glimpse of what's on "the other side" of your defenses.

I've also introduced a strategy that will be used throughout the chapters in this middle part: as I do in Exercises 2 and 4 above, I'll be asking you to step outside of your comfort zone in order to expose and challenge your defenses. As discussed in greater detail in Chapter Thirteen, genuine psychological growth is most likely to happen when we *choose* to do something other than what comes naturally and most easily to us. Defense mechanisms are built-in mental habits; in order to grow, we have to do what we may not want to do in order to challenge them.

This strategy for growth will be the focus of the final part of the book, but throughout the chapters in this middle section, I'll be suggesting ways for you to begin challenging the mental status quo.

F I V E

Displacement and Reaction Formation

Don't take it out on me!
– Said by most of us, at one time or another

Displacement

Have you ever said the above words to someone else, or had them said to you? They perfectly describe the process of displacement. You have a feeling–say, you're angry because your boss yelled at you at work–but because you feel unable to express that anger for fear of losing your job, you direct the feeling at somebody else, someone who has likely done nothing to incur your anger. That person feels unjustly treated, recognizes the problem and tells you not to make her the scapegoat for your anger.

"Don't take it out on me!"

The feeling remains conscious but is directed away from the person who inspired it. This is an instance where the defense mechanism is not especially powerful, unlike denial where the feeling may be entirely absent from your awareness. In displacement, the truth may lie very close to the surface; many people, if told not to "take out" their bad mood on a loved one, will eventually recognize what they've been doing and apologize. You can probably think of examples from your own experience.

The Usefulness of Displacement

Let me offer a different kind of example, one that I've heard repeated in various ways from different clients over the years. This type of displacement is much farther from consciousness, reflecting a more powerful defense mechanism at work. It also illustrates the positive value of defenses, how we need them to cope effectively with certain situations. Here's the general outline of the story:

In the middle of the night, a new mother awakens to her infant's hunger cries and gets out of bed to feed it. As she sits in the rocking chair, nursing her baby, she feels a blissful kind of communion with the child. She may marvel at the power of her maternal love, and how she hasn't experienced anything like it before. She might think to herself that she's never felt happier or more satisfied with her life. Her baby, finally sated, drops off to sleep again; she places it in the crib, returning to her own bedroom.

At the sight of her husband in bed, slumbering unaware, she may at first feel a little sorry for him, that he's missing out on this wonderful closeness. If she finds herself unable to fall back asleep, she might begin to feel a little resentment toward him instead. If the baby once again wakes up and she has to drag herself from bed one more time, the way she feels toward her husband may begin to change.

He's so lucky that he doesn't have to get up in the middle of the night like I do. Tomorrow he'll probably feel rested while I'll be dragging myself around all day in a state of exhaustion. It's totally unfair, the way the burden of breast-feeding falls entirely on the mother! I'd like to wake him up right now, just so he'll know what it feels like.

By this point, she's so full of anger and resentment that falling back to sleep may be difficult.

While there's some truth to all of this mother's thoughts, it doesn't explain the degree of anger. Some new mothers ask their husbands to give the baby a bottle for one of those middle-of-the-night feedings, but it doesn't necessarily mitigate the anger. Even couples who share child-care duties more evenly may quietly nurse their resentment, each one feeling that his or her share of the responsibility is lopsidedly large. In addition to the stories I've heard from clients, I've talked with friends about their experience as they became mothers and fathers. I have three children of my own. As far as I can tell, occasional anger and resentment just seem to be a part of parenting.

So what's going on here? The mothers (or sometimes the fathers giving a bottle) feel resentful about having to wake up and lose sleep in order to take care of the baby. They don't realize it—and they might deny it if someone suggested as much—but they are angry about the amount of deprivation involved in parenthood, how difficult it is to sacrifice sleep and other personal needs to those of the baby. It's neither rational nor fair, but they feel resentment toward their own child. Nothing in our cultural messages or the parenting books we read prepares us for this anger; on the contrary, all the sentimental depictions of parenting suggest that we will feel only love for our infants, that people who hate their babies are very bad people, of course—child abusers and the like.

In my experience, you can't avoid a certain degree of anger or resentment when you have an infant. It's an enormous responsibility and a huge sacrifice of personal freedom; even when a baby has been longed for, the lack of sleep, day after day, takes its toll. Instead of resenting the helpless and demanding infant who is actually responsible for that lack of sleep, new mothers often resent their husbands instead. This is a perfect example of displacement. A feeling aroused by and directed at one person is felt to be unacceptable or dangerous, and so is displaced onto another.

The father is much better able than an infant to cope with the anger directed at him, even if he feels it's unfair. In my view, it's one of the more important and overlooked roles of a father, to absorb his wife's anger when she can't and shouldn't direct it at their baby. The defense mechanism of displacement allows her to shift the focus of a powerful feeling that might overwhelm and harm an infant, directing it instead toward someone (hopefully) more capable of coping with it.

How Displacement May Damage Relationships

A reverse example of displacement shows its potential to damage relationships when used in a less beneficial way. The father of a newborn finds himself "pushed aside" by the baby and may feel jealous of the attention it receives from his wife; their normal sex life has probably suffered for a while now and may have come to a complete halt since the birth. While rejoicing in fatherhood on one level, he may unconsciously feel angry and resentful at all the deprivation involved – angry at his wife for "abandoning" him and resentful of the baby for usurping his place at the center of her affections.

At the office, he may become more and more irritable with his colleagues, who find him uncharacteristically difficult to work with. Loss of sleep (even if he's not the one getting up with the baby) only makes matters worse. When something goes wrong – a deadline is missed, say, or a project falls short of expectations – he might even "lose it" with a co-worker and become abusive. Because he feels unable to express his anger toward his wife and child, he displaces it onto his colleagues. People at work feel as if he is "taking it out" on them, though they may not be able to identify the exact nature of the "it." If this behavior goes on for long, it may seriously damage his work relationships in lasting ways.

Reaction Formation

This defense mechanism involves turning an unacceptable feeling or impulse into its exact opposite. In the media, the Republican politician or religious conservative with rabidly anti-gay positions who gets caught engaging in illicit homosexual behavior is often cited (mistakenly, as I'll explain) as a case of reaction formation. Famous examples include

George Rekers (who hired a young man from Rentboy.com to "carry his luggage" throughout Europe); Pastor Ted Haggard of Colorado Springs, who engaged in a three-year sexual relationship with his "masseur"; and former Senator Larry Craig of Idaho, caught playing footsy with an undercover cop in the Minneapolis airport's men's room.

In discussing such scandals on an episode of *Dr. Drew* in 2011, one clinical psychologist incorrectly described them as a textbook case of reaction formation, where the individual adopts one virulent position in public that expresses hatred for another part of himself. But reaction formation, like all defense mechanisms, is an *unconscious process*. If a man is *conscious* of having a desire for sexual relations with another man while becoming an advocate for the sanctity of traditional marriage, his behavior would more accurately be described as hypocrisy.

On the other hand, if a different man – say, a pastor or a politician – adopts an anti-gay platform and persecutes gays, or if a young man likes to beat up other men as they emerge from gay bars but isn't consciously aware of his sexual attraction to them, then it would be an example of true reaction formation.

The Reformed Smoker

A more familiar example is the intense disgust and intolerance for cigarette smoke felt by many people who have successfully quit smoking. Before they decided to give it up, the taste and aroma of burning tobacco used to delight them. When they first attempted to break their habit, it might have felt like a form of torture to be around someone smoking, in part because it smelled so good. Months later, after they have truly broken the habit, they may develop a strong aversion to that same smell – a reaction formation.

Here again, we see how a defense mechanism might be a benefit. Although on some level such people may long to resume smoking, the disgust they consciously feel keeps them from slipping back into a destructive habit. If you've met with this type of reformed smoker, you might have felt irritated, wondering why the person had to make such a fuss, even ostracizing somebody else for doing just what the ex-smoker used to do. The intensity of this aversion is a telltale sign that a defense mechanism is at work.

Reaction Formation as a Part of Character

Otto Fenichel long ago noted[13] that reaction formation as a defense mechanism often becomes integrated into one's personality type or style, acting as a continual, ongoing kind of defense against a large part of one's emotional life (as opposed to say, denial, which is usually focused on one specific fact or feeling). A familiar cultural stereotype is the prude whose prim demeanor wards off powerfully threatening sexual impulses.

As a therapist, I've more often encountered reaction formation as an aspect of character when anger and aggression are the issue. For example, a young woman named Nicole began treatment because of profound depression, impulsive and uncontrollable drug usage and self-injurious types of behavior. In particular, she would often slice open portions of her arms and legs with a razor blade. Nicole often told me she wanted very much to be a "good person"; she thought of herself as especially kind-hearted. She worked at an animal shelter and spoke with feeling about her love for animals.

Early in her treatment, Nicole told me the following story, about a grade school experience from her childhood. Some of the other students found a wounded bird on the playground; they began to poke it with sticks and torture it in other ways. Nicole tried to rescue the bird, begging the other children to stop. During her session—years later—she wept as she related the story. She didn't understand how people

---

[13]Otto Fenichel. *The Psychoanalytic Theory of Neuroses* (New York: Norton, 1945), p. 151.

could be so heartless and cruel. Through her tears, she told me that those children had been laughing as they poked the poor bird with their sticks.

As we learned over time, Nicole struggled with powerful feelings of explosive anger, and some sadistic urges that she directed at her own body rather than other people. Because she found this sadistic side of her character unbearable and frightening, she had developed a reaction formation to it—a "good person" self-image that embodied the very opposite kinds of feelings. She loved animals, devoting herself to their welfare; she condemned the exercise of cruelty in others.

Over the years, I've often heard new clients say about themselves, "Whatever my difficulties, at least I'm a good person," or "I really want to be a good person." In actual fact, they may have devoted themselves to charities, church work, public service and various other types of volunteer work; within their own world, they may be viewed as Good Samaritans or even saints. Many people find great meaning in such philanthropic work, but when they rely upon it as *proof* of their own goodness, when they place undue emphasis on appearing a certain way and being viewed as a "good person" by others, it usually means they unconsciously struggle with very different kinds of feelings, especially anger and hatred.

Reaction Formation at Work along with Displacement

Often, these "good" people find more acceptable ways to express their aggression, *displacing* it onto strangers or into social causes, rather than directing it at their loved ones. Animal rights activists or environmentalists who engage in acts of great domestic violence in the name of their organizations, for example. The so-called "bleeding heart" liberal who rabidly hates and vilifies conservatives. This is not to denigrate their positions or to trivialize their values; rather, it shows how one's "goodness" and devotion to a compassionate cause can function as a character defense while at the same time furthering an ideal.

This is especially true when depression is a major issue. While there are different types of depression, one serious form results from profound unconscious anger–aggressive feelings that are both frightening and unacceptable to the depressed person. The devoted church-goer, for instance, who strives to emulate Christ's loving compassion and battles a lifelong depression resulting from "anger turned inward." Because such people can't bear to face their own aggression, they develop a reaction formation to it–a "good person" identity; they may ward off the awareness of anger or hatred but as a result, fall prey to depression.

Reaction Formation and Shame

Where profound shame is a problem, you sometimes see a reaction formation to it in the form of *shamelessness*. Because the word shameless has become a favorite attack word in politics (*e.g.*, "In putting forward these supposed facts, the candidate proves himself to be a shameless liar"), we need to be clear: shameless, in the psychodynamic sense, is not the same thing as feeling unashamed or indifferent in cases where someone else thinks you *ought* to feel ashamed. Shameless means to flaunt a particular behavior, to publicly express defiance of some social norm or value; in no way is the person indifferent, nor is he actually proud. Rather, the shameless behavior embodies his reaction formation to unbearable shame.

One of my clients, Eliza, worked as a pole dancer in a men's club as well as at private parties; she was not a prostitute and didn't engage in sex for money. In situations where she expected (rightly or wrongly) to encounter judgment about her line of work, Eliza often found a way to make an aggressive announcement about her job, as if to "shove it" in the person's face. She unconsciously felt a great deal of shame, not about her job so much as about *herself* and the ways she was psychologically damaged; she feared being truly *seen* by other people and judged by them as being defective. Her aggressive posture of indifference to such judgment embodied a reaction formation to her underlying sense of shame.

As I'll discuss in Chapter Eleven, *Defenses against Shame*, many forms of narcissistic self-display can be understood as a type of reaction formation. When unconscious feelings of shame dominate a person, she dreads being truly seen. She fears appearing defective or damaged, even deformed, and therefore strives to appear beautiful instead, eliciting admiration.

Narcissists present us with an idealized, false image of themselves and clamor for admiring attention, in order to prevent us from seeing the damaged, shame-ridden self inside. It's an example of reaction formation: the unconscious fear of being seen becomes the conscious desire to be watched.

What to Look For

Once again: the *What to Look For* section in each chapter explains how the defense mechanisms under discussion play out in relation to our primary psychological concerns (Chapter Two). Each chapter in Part II will include such a discussion before the exercises, with specific reference to *Need and Dependency*, *Emotions* and *Self-Esteem*.

Need and Dependency

As discussed in the last chapter, people sometimes turn to sub-stances – food, alcohol and illicit drugs – rather than to people, because *things* are more predictable than human beings. If you know someone who struggles with substance issues and has a hard time sustaining close relationships, or if you consider yourself "addicted" in one way or another, then unbearable neediness of an interpersonal kind may be an underlying issue. The need is *displaced* from the true object of desire (a person) onto an object. Readers who responded most to **Group 1** and **Group 2** statements might rely on this defense in different ways.

I previously described this process as one where a need is *denied* and *repressed*. Once again, we see how a particular psychological dynamic can be thought of as one defense mechanism from a certain point of view and a different defense mechanism from another. The label is not as important as the underlying pain we're trying to avoid. Many people find it almost unbearable to need someone else, or to feel frustrated when they can't immediately have what they want from the other.

These issues often become a focus of psychotherapy; if this discussion strikes a chord, you may want to think about your own childhood, the ways it shaped the person you have become and the psychological defenses you use. Maybe extremely unreliable, rejecting or emotionally distant parents made you feel it was unsafe to depend too much on other people.

Disgust sometimes reflects a reaction formation at work, especially when it's expressed in an intense or dramatic way. In evolutionary terms, disgust developed as means of protecting our species from substances that might contaminate or injure us – for example, our reaction of disgust to feces. This inbuilt mechanism can be enlisted in the service of psychological defense, to ward off desires or attractions we fear may "contaminate" or injure us if we let them in.

As discussed earlier, homophobia is the classic example, but in any situation where a strong feeling of disgust or aversion comes up, it might be a defense. People who find sexual desire to be frightening may ward off their own impulses by becoming puritanical and disapproving, expressing disgust at modern sexual behavior, or even feeling repelled by their own sexual organs. It's one thing to believe that promiscuity involves all sorts of emotional and physical risks; it's quite another to feel *scorn* and *revulsion* for people less able or willing to control their urges. If you feel that way, chances are it has had a stunting effect on your own marriage or romantic relationships. Readers who related most to **Group 1** statements should pay attention.

A man who expresses contempt for weakness and for overly needy people may be warding off his own wish to be taken care of. A career woman who feels superior to and scornful of the stay-at-home wife may unconsciously long for just such an experience as part of her own marriage. In all of these cases where a reaction formation is at work, you will notice a particular intensity of response that seems unusual and may surprise or even offend other people.

Emotions

Those of us who have a hard time expressing anger with someone we're close to will often displace it onto someone or something else, as described earlier in this chapter. What you will notice, either in yourself or other people, is an intensity that seems inappropriate to the situation at hand. Someone might say to you, "I don't see what you're getting so angry about"; you might feel that a friend's reaction seems "over the top." Sometimes, the anger may actually be appropriate, where it's a question of "the straw that broke the camel's back"; but where there's an intensity of response that seems unusual, it might instead reflect displacement from the true object of that anger – a spouse, friend or family member.

In keeping with the "good person" example from earlier in the chapter, extreme or excessive "niceness" often reflects a reaction for-mation to hostility (not to be confused with calculating phoniness or deliberate insincerity). Sometimes we use the words "cloying" or "saccharine sweet" to describe such behavior. "To kill someone with kindness" also gets at the way a display of one emotion may actually mask its opposite. With a person who expresses herself in this manner, you may even feel that she's actually being hostile in some way you can't put your finger on. Sometimes this may be a conscious aim but often such a person may have no idea what she actually feels. This would apply to the reader who related most to **Group 3** statements.

Look for situations where your reaction to what someone else has expressed, or another person's reaction to you, is jarringly different from what seems to be happening on the surface. Do co-workers regularly respond to your behavior in ways that surprise you? Do you often find yourself saying, "But I didn't mean it that way!" The other person might have reacted to the *unconscious communication* of a feeling that is the exact opposite of what you consciously intended.

Self-esteem

People who struggle with feelings of shame often displace it onto their personal exterior or their possessions. The excruciating sense of being damaged or defective *inside* may show up as an excessive concern that one is physically ugly, dresses badly, drives an "inferior" car, has an embarrassing apartment, etc. In other words, the shame is displaced from the inside (the intrinsic person) to the outside (his appearance or possessions). If you related most to **Group 5** statements, this might apply to you. I'll have more to say about this dynamic in Chapter Eleven and narcissistic defenses against shame.

You might know someone who's always asking for reassurance about his looks, or makes self-deprecating jokes that beg for contradiction. Such behavior places strains on a friendship because continually having to provide such reassurance can become wearing. Maybe you feel "insecure" about how you dress and crave compliments from other people. While we can conceptualize these feelings and behaviors in various ways, whatever we name the defense, the shame is unbearable. It shows up in an intense preoccupation with personal appearances and receiving compliments from our friends and loved ones.

As with my client Eliza, people who develop a reaction formation to shame may appear defiantly shameless. Listening to a friend insist he doesn't feel bad about something that happened, you may have thought to yourself, *If you really don't feel bad, then why keep going on and on about it?* Once again, it's the dynamic conveyed in that quote from Shakespeare, now part of our everyday lexicon: "The lady doth protest too much, methinks." The reaction formation to shame appears as a kind of defiance of convention that feels overdone.

By now, it should have become clear that *unusual or inappropriate intensity* is one of the telltale signs that a defense mechanism may be at work. Be on the lookout for it, in yourself as well as in others. At the same time, I don't want to homogenize human behavior and exclude the element of passion from what we consider "normal." Sometimes hatred and anger accompany our highest ideals when we find those ideals betrayed. We may feel contempt when we see our standards flouted, especially in unthinking or careless ways. If a social stricture appears especially petty or small-minded, we may be right to express public scorn or defiance.

One possible way to tell the difference: if you often find yourself engaged in mental self-justification, if you regularly have conversations with people "in your head" where you attempt to prove that they are *wrong* and you are *right*, it may be a sign that you're attempting to justify a psychological defense. It could be a displacement or a reaction formation that you're trying to bolster, but it could be some other defense mechanism as well. I'll discuss the issue of self-justification in greater detail in Part III, *Disarming Your Defenses*.

EXERCISES

1. Have you ever taken your anger out on someone who didn't deserve it?

   • Who or what was the actual cause of that anger? Don't be satisfied with explanations like "I was just in a bad mood." Bad moods aren't random events without meaning and there are often very good explanations for them.

   • Can you identify the reasons why you didn't express that anger directly? It could have been proximity—the innocent person may simply have been in the wrong place at the wrong time; or it might have felt inappropriate or dangerous to express anger toward the actual target of that feeling.

- Now imagine yourself expressing the anger toward the real object of it. Develop this fantasy as fully as you can, elaborating the scene and the interactions between you. It might help to speak aloud, as if the person were there in the room with you.

- Did you feel uncomfortable or anxious about expressing your anger? If so, it will tell you something about how well you tolerate the experience of anger and hatred.

2. Review your attitudes about hostility:

- Do you feel that anger is a purely destructive emotion or does it sometimes have a value?

- Do you feel there are appropriate and inappropriate ways to express anger? How would you differentiate them?

3. Do you find yourself intensely preoccupied with food, alcohol or some other drug, or do you feel a strong drive to accumulate material objects? If so:

- On some occasion when you feel such a craving, instead of gratifying it right away, sit down with your journal and write down a description of how it feels to want or desire the particular thing.

- Be detailed and thorough; push yourself to be as specific as possible. Do you notice any other emotions or urges coming up as you write? Describe those feelings in detail, too. Try to wait as long as possible before gratifying the urge.

4. Do you have any strong reactions of disgust or revulsion that most other people don't seem to share? Reaction formation is one of the less common defenses mechanisms, so don't be surprised if the answer is *no*. But if you did answer *yes*:

- Using sentences that begin with the words "I'm disgusted by X because..." or "I find X repulsive because...," write a detailed description of exactly what it is that arouses such disgust or revulsion. **Complete this part of the exercise *before* reading on.**

- Now re-write those sentences, replacing the words *disgusted by* and *repulsive* with *attracted to* and *attractive* respectively. You'll likely find this exercise absurd; the idea of feeling attraction instead of disgust may strike you as preposterous.

- Pay close attention to this response and just how powerfully you reject the idea of attraction. Contempt and ridicule, in particular, might mean you feel a powerful need to bolster your defenses.

5. Have you ever felt intensely defiant about flouting some widely accepted code of behavior? It might have been the rules of an organization or possibly the wishes of your own family. Did you think to yourself, *I refuse to let them make me feel guilty about this!*

   - It may simply be that you're an independent spirit who refuses to submit to social norms that seem wrong or unfair.

   - On the other hand, if you feel the need to make a big show of your "indifference" to judgment, or if you expend a lot of mental energy justifying your defiance, arguing with imaginary critics in your head in order to prove them wrong, it may indicate the presence of deeply painful and unconscious guilt (or shame); you may be warding it off with this reaction formation of shamelessness or defiant indifference.

   - Suspend disbelief for a moment, quiet the voice in your head that insists on your own point of view and entertain the idea that you really care a great deal more than you say. You don't have to admit this to anyone else. Try very hard to see the other side of the argument in your head. How do you feel as a result?

Now What?

Your answers to the first two questions should help bring your attitudes about anger into sharper focus; like most people, you may feel uncomfortable with feeling and expressing hostility. This book takes the view that anger is a normal part of human relationships (see Chapter Three, pp. 36-37); if you feel especially uneasy with that idea, you may be relying on a defense mechanism to protect you. Pay attention to the way you feel around other people who express anger.

The final question introduces an approach I'll discuss throughout the book but especially in Chapter Thirteen: recognizing the way we rely on mental arguments or repetitive thoughts that insist on a certain point of view in order to *justify* a defense mechanism. In the coming week, pay attention to your thoughts to see whether you can identify this process as work. Almost everybody mentally justifies their defenses at one time or another.

SIX

Splitting

The more you love someone,
The more he make you crazy.
The more you love someone,
The more you wishing him dead!
– From the Broadway musical, *Avenue Q*

Of the defense mechanisms to be discussed in this book, splitting is perhaps the most difficult to understand. Unlike denial and repression, the idea of splitting hasn't fully entered the cultural mainstream, so we don't have familiar references from daily speech, books or movies to provide us with an easy entrée into the concept. It's also more difficult to recognize within ourselves than some of the other defenses.

In order to make splitting easier to grasp, my strategy here differs somewhat from my approach in other chapters. I'll talk first about the emotional issues that splitting is most often meant to address—ambivalence and strong feelings of hatred—then go on to show how splitting as a defense seeks to *simplify* the former and *eliminate awareness* of the latter.

And because splitting is easier to identify *outside*, within the broader social context, this chapter will include more examples from politics and the public realm, eventually applying what has been learned to individual psychology.

The Two Types of Ambivalence

The funny, insightful song lyrics from *Avenue Q* that head this chapter are delivered by a young Japanese-American woman (hence the grammatical oddness of its lyrics), puzzling over the age-old problem of romantic passion—that strong feelings of love sometimes give way to murderous rage. Although most visible with intense emotional bonds, the experience of opposing feelings (love and hatred) is a part of almost all of our important relationships. Coping with the reality of such *ambivalence* is part of the human struggle—how to avoid hurting people we care about during those emotional flare-ups when we briefly want to *kill* them.

The word *ambivalence* is more commonly used in its other sense: an inability to make up our minds, or feeling unsure about what we would most like to do. It means being pulled by our desires in more than one direction. If you've experienced such ambivalence—that is, had a hard time making up your mind about which option to choose or what to do when you felt pulled in different directions—you know how distressing it can be, how difficult to bear.

When we feel uncomfortably ambivalent, we usually want to *resolve* the uncertainty about what to do as quickly as possible. Over the years, many different clients have told me they couldn't stop thinking about a situation where they felt ambivalent, often "obsessing" over it until they made up their minds. Maybe you've had a similar experience. Sometimes we make a choice, any choice, simply to put an end to the uncertainty because we can't bear it any longer.

As the neurologist Robert Burton has noted, ambiguity or confusion is so difficult for many of us to bear that we instead retreat from it into a feeling of *certainty*, believing we know something without any doubts, even when we actually don't and often can't know.[14] Strictly

---

[14]Robert Burton. *On Being Certain: Believing You Are Right Even When You're Not* (New York: St. Martin's Press, 2008).

codified forms of morality, rigid belief systems and dogmatic narrow-mindedness all protect us from the pain of uncertainty.

F. Scott Fitzgerald once said: "The test of a first-rate intelligence is the ability to hold two opposing ideas in mind at the same time and still retain the ability to function."[15] Whether it actually is a question of intelligence (as opposed to psychological maturity or emotional capacity) most of us have a hard time doing what Fitzgerald described. Instead, we tend to reject one of those opposing ideas and take refuge in the other. This process is especially visible in the political arena, where many people have absolute, simplistic and immutable beliefs about how to address thorny social problems.

Facing complexity, feeling uncertain about what to do, seeing and sympathizing with opposing perspectives—it's a highly uncomfortable place to be. Those of us who have trouble with such discomfort often resort to black-and-white thinking instead. Rather than feeling uncertain or ambivalent, struggling with areas of gray, we reduce that complexity to *either/or*.

We may define one idea or point of view as *bad* (black) and reject it, aligning ourselves with the *good* (white) perspective. Feelings of anger and self-righteousness often accompany this process, bolstering our conviction that we are in the right and the other side in the wrong. Ambiguity and compromise are out of the question because they plunge us back into the painful realm of ambivalence.

Black-and-white thinking reflects the psychological defense mechanism known as *splitting*. When we feel unable to tolerate the tension and confusion aroused by complexity, we "resolve" that complexity by *splitting* it into two simplified and opposing parts, usually aligning ourselves with one of them and rejecting the other. As a result, we may feel a sort of comfort in believing we know something with absolute

---

[15] F. Scott Fitzgerald, *The Crackup*. (New York: New Directions Publishing, 1945).

certainty; at the same time, we've over-simplified a complex issue, robbing it of its richness and vitality.

If you've ever found yourself arguing with someone who believes he knows the truth with absolute certainty, you'll understand what a frustrating, dead-end experience it can be.

The Problem of Hatred

In a related manner, we make use of splitting to cope with our emotional lives as well. Ambivalence in its second sense – simultaneous and contradictory attitudes or feelings such as love and hatred – presents an even greater challenge than to tolerate opposing points of view. Have you ever had a traumatic fight with a loved one – a romantic partner, friend or family member – and felt in the heat of the moment that you never wanted to speak to that person again? Following some major outburst, did you feel absolutely certain that a relationship was *finished*, only to change your mind about it the following day?

It's difficult to bear with temporary feelings of hatred for someone we love, especially since, in our culture, hatred is largely viewed as an unacceptable emotion. Popular depictions of human nature, to be found in children's books, family-oriented TV shows, politically-correct school units on various social issues, etc. regularly delete hatred, or vilify its expression. We learn that hatred is a feeling we're not supposed to have, despite the many places you can see it regularly expressed: by religious zealots, politicians, racists, war-mongers, etc.

It's especially unacceptable in our close personal relationships, even though most of us, at one time or another, have said something like, "I was so furious, I could've killed him." You might want to object that it's just "a way of talking," not seriously meant. We have no intention of actually committing homicide, of course; but why does the idea of murder even come up? Why not express the emotion in some other way entirely? Even if it's on an unconscious level, most people have experienced murderous rage at one time or another.

Few of us want to acknowledge feelings of hatred for a parent, child, spouse or a close friend, although it seems much easier to admit you feel that way about a sibling. Especially in childhood, before we're fully "civilized," physical violence commonly breaks out between children in the same family; even in adulthood, it's common for siblings to have stormy relationships, to erupt in anger at holiday gatherings or bear grudges against each other for years. If you haven't felt that way yourself, you've undoubtedly known other people who have. The hatred may be so intense, so unbearable that brothers and sisters may break off relations entirely.

We also find our own hatred acceptable when it seems well-justified, when somebody has hurt us deeply. Especially if there's malice involved on the other side, or callous insensitivity, we believe that it's okay to hate. Ever feel enraged when some other driver "stole" the parking space you'd been waiting for? Ever want to punch someone who deliberately cut in line in front of you? Ever want to throttle your partner or spouse for making a derogatory remark about you in front of your friends?

In our close relationships, hatred can be deeply painful and disruptive. When it overpowers us, we may strike out and inflict pain, hurting people we care about. You've probably had the experience of lashing out during an argument and saying words you later came to regret. In the heat of the moment, you may have felt that you hated the other person and wanted your relationship to end; you may even have said so in cruel and abusive language.

Over the years, many clients have told me of discord in their relationships; I've learned that, when overcome with hatred, it's not at all unusual for people to say "Fuck you!" or even "Fuck off and die!" to their partners.

The Universality of Hatred

In my practice, clients sometimes correct me if I use the word hatred to describe their feelings: "Maybe I feel angry, but hatred is kind of strong. I don't think I feel hate." They usually believe hatred is a *bad* emotion to be feeling; it means there's something *wrong* with you. Hatred is one of those feelings self-help books and spiritual guides will often teach you how to *transcend* or *overcome,* as if we could forever rid ourselves of the emotion.

But turn on the evening news and you'll see daily atrocities committed in Africa, the brutal suppression of dissent throughout the Mideast, heinous crimes committed in our own country, countless acts of vengeance by corrupt regimes or rebel armies all over the world. Every day, hatred is expressed by people everywhere.

If you watch the reality TV shows, you'll see this aspect of human nature vividly and shamelessly expressed: attention-hungry guests, goaded to provide spectacle for the TV viewing audience, will say vicious things to people whom they supposedly love. Hatred is a fact of life, and coping with it, learning to inhibit its expression, especially in our most important relationships, is part of becoming civilized.

Just as the splitting involved in black-and-white thinking may "resolve" the ambiguity of opposing ideas, so can splitting help us cope with the problem of ambivalence in our relationships. In the emotional arena, splitting means to divide up the loving and hating impulses and keep them entirely separate. Often this means directing the hatred at a person other than the one it's truly meant for.

In the previous chapter about displacement, I gave the example of a new mother who resents her husband rather than her infant; such displacement depends upon this kind of emotional splitting. The mother has *split apart* her ambivalence about this demanding baby; she relishes the loving, contented feelings and *displaces* her hostility from the baby onto her husband.

As you try to understand defense mechanisms and how they work, assigning names and isolating the exact processes is less important than recognizing the pain they're meant to resolve. It's difficult and painful to have mixed emotions (feelings of love and hatred) for *anyone* who is close to us, and especially so if it's the helpless infant we may have always longed for.

The Story of Alexis

One of my clients, Alexis, struggled with ambivalence in both senses of the word. At the time she began treatment, she'd been dating two different men for months – Steve and Brian – usually not at the same time but rather in rotation. First she'd decide she wanted to be with Steve; then she'd change her mind, drop Steve and switch to Brian. She couldn't make up her mind.

At the beginning of each new stint with one or the other, Alexis would feel "in love" and believe she was happy (but with lingering doubts about whether she'd made the right choice); when a conflict that made her angry or frustrated inevitably came up, she'd quickly decide she'd made a mistake, drop the current boyfriend and re-connect with the one she'd earlier rejected.

Alexis couldn't cope with the reality of a relationship. Our partners inevitably do things that annoy or frustrate us; whenever she felt anger or frustration, she took it as evidence that she'd made the wrong choice. Hers was an idealized view of love as a perfect state, untainted by the other complicating emotions which she would split off and reject at the moment she felt them.

But bearing the anger and sometimes even the hatred that comes up in relationships, not behaving in destructive ways that hurt our loved ones at those moments, is what allows us to sustain intimacy with another person over many years. This applies to our friendships and family ties, as well.

As I'll discuss in Part III, bearing this type of ambivalence means learning to experience an emotion without it overwhelming you, and understanding that all feelings are temporary. Tolerating ambivalence means being able to think and truly believe: *I may hate you right now, I might want to rip your guts out, but I know this feeling will pass and I'll eventually feel my love for you again.*

Useful vs. Excessive Splitting

Excessive splitting can make relationships difficult and unstable. Maybe you know someone who repeatedly starts and ends romantic relationships, or who regularly makes and drops new friends. If you can't tolerate the reality of mixed emotions, you'll have a hard time sustaining close human contact.

On the other hand, splitting often allows us to sustain and protect our relationships. Having other outlets for our angry feelings means we can shield our loved ones from those emotions. If we have legitimate reasons for feeling angry, it's important to communicate that anger (in constructive ways) to our friends, family members and colleagues, but it's not such a good idea to blast them with the full force of our anger in the heat of the moment.

One of the helpful functions of society is to provide us with outlets for our anger – to identify places where it's okay to feel and express (split-off) aggression, even hatred. Consider the uses of professional sports, for example, where most spectators identify with one team or competitor and wish to crush the opponent. Not only does this provide a needed outlet for competitive urges, but it also allows us to channel many aggressive feelings away from our intimate relationships and express them in a safer context.

Warfare, with an identified enemy combatant, may also serve the same function, providing a sanctioned outlet for our aggression. In times of war, splitting becomes powerfully evident: people at home come together more easily, put differences aside and unite against the common enemy. For a time, it can create a sense of domestic harmony and unification, especially important when confronting an existential threat from the outside.

But people who rely heavily on this type of defense may have trouble *without* such an outlet for aggression. In the 1979 film *The Great Santini*, for example, Colonel Bull Meechum returns from deployment abroad and proceeds to terrorize his family. He later admits to his friend Virgil that it's difficult to be a warrior during peacetime. He needs the sanctioned outlet for his aggression, allowing him to split it off and direct it away from his loved ones. Without such an outlet, he steadily brutalizes his wife and four children.

Perhaps, like me, you've attended your child's sporting events and seen one particular father who's overly invested in victory for his daughter's team, who becomes hostile and abusive toward the ref when calls go the wrong way. He likely struggles with hatred, attempts to split off and channel it into sport, but still finds the feeling unmanageable. Sometimes "road rage" can reflect the process of splitting: while in theory, it's much safer to direct your rage at strangers, it can also get you into trouble if that other driver gets equally enraged because you cut him off in traffic!

You can also see splitting used by the extremely angry environmentalist who I described in the last chapter, the hostile animal rights activist who fights to protect innocent creatures or the environment with intense hatred, directed at ruthless corporate polluters or evil laboratory scientists. They may feel and often are justified in their anger; but when splitting is excessive, their worldview becomes simplistic: cartoon-like bad guys versus the pure and innocent victim.

Perceptions of and attitudes toward loved ones may also become two-dimensional. People who rely on splitting may become overly "nice" in their intimate relationships; on a personal level, they may come across as artificial or saccharine. They have split off their aggressive feelings and chosen an outlet they find more acceptable, but the price they pay is a lack of genuine intimacy in their friendships, as well as in their family and romantic relationships.

Splitting Our Perceptions of Other People

When splitting is active, it often affects our ability to perceive other people accurately. In the example above, the overly zealous activist sees the issue of animal rights or protecting the environment in black-and-white, even moralistic terms; as a result, those on the other side often become caricatures—ruthless corporate bigwigs or cruel scientists—rather than three-dimensional people. As discussed earlier in this chapter, we find it easier to accept our hatred if we feel it's justified; sometimes we unconsciously distort our own perceptions as a way to justify feelings of hatred.

In order to find a safe outlet for our hostile feelings, then, we may perceive the world in very clear terms of good and bad: helpless, innocent animals we adore and the bad people who exploit them; the pristine environment and the evildoers who pollute it. We hate those bad people and they *deserve* it. In time of war, governments make use of this type of splitting via propaganda, in order to convince us that the other side is *evil*. Consider films made during World War II, full of cartoon Nazis.

Hate those people—they deserve it!

Heroes in those war films from the 1940s are often as two-dimensional as the evil Nazis they battle, uncomplicated in their goodness—fearless, idealistic, full of love for their country and ready to die for it. You rarely hear a politician today speak of our soldiers in uniform as other than models of courage and self-sacrifice. Viewing the world in terms of black and white, of good versus evil, reflects the process of splitting. It takes hold of a complex, ambiguous reality and makes it simple for the purposes of defense, be it an individual psychological defense mechanism, or one of national defense, mobilizing a population's hatred during time of war.

Splitting Under Extreme Stress

Even people who don't rely heavily on splitting as a defense mechanism may resort to splitting under extreme distress, when their normal coping mechanisms let them down. Denial or repression might work for a time, but then intense emotion may break through and splitting acts as a sort of back-up defense. I can explain this process more clearly with an example.

The nephew of my client Chloe fell in with a group of drug dealers and was brutally murdered by them. The killers were apprehended but came to trial only after several years. As the trial approached, anticipating the horrors they would hear from the witness stand, Chloe and her family pulled together as a kind of support group. They set up a schedule to ensure that at least one family member would be present at all times. Ordinary events and obligations fell by the wayside; life revolved around the upcoming trial.

During this period, Chloe's family became devoted to the cause of justice for the murdered boy who, as is so often the case in such situations, had become a much better person in memory than he'd been in real life. This family pursued their cause with an almost religious zeal: seeing the killers sent to jail forever became the sole focus of their lives. Past grievances and irritations between family members were set aside. Most of us can understand how this might happen; most of us would probably react the same way.

Not long before the trial began, a friend made the mistake of complaining about Chloe's brother—for very good reasons, as it later came out, though Chloe couldn't see it at the time. She turned on her friend and severed relations, accusing her of treating the brother "viciously" when in truth the brother was entirely at fault. Chloe's friend became a very "bad" person, an enemy who had to be exiled.

Like a nation under stress during time of war, Chloe's family pulled together. The murdered nephew had been *good*, their family was *loving*, and anyone not entirely supportive was *bad*. Chloe's friend became a malicious enemy she had to vanquish. Because the pain and horror of the upcoming trial had placed so much stress upon her, she could no longer tolerate ambiguous, ambivalent situations: she couldn't bear to think that the brother whom she loved had also behaved badly toward her friend.

Months later, after the trial had ended and the murderers were convicted, when Chloe no longer had to cope with such extreme stress, she came to understand her friend's point-of-view and mended the friendship. She recovered the more nuanced view of her brother she normally held. But during that awful time, before and during the trial, she had to cope with so much pain that a nuanced, ambivalent view over-taxed her emotional capacities.

What to Look For

Extremes of good and bad are the hallmark of splitting, along with big shifts from highly positive to extremely negative emotions about important relationships; you'll see big fluctuations in the perception of other people, who may move abruptly from pedestal to trash heap overnight. Black and white thinking is the order of the day.

Need and Dependency

Men and women who have trouble bearing the inevitable frustration that comes up when they depend upon other people may fall in and out of love quickly, first believing in the perfection of a new partner, then rejecting him or her as worthless. Like my client Alexis, you may struggle with the reality of mixed emotions, "resolving" your ambivalence by getting rid of the romantic partner who just disappointed you or made you angry. Readers who identified with **Group 4** statements would be likely to rely on this kind of splitting.

You might see a similar pattern in your friendships: maybe you think uncritically about certain people you admire while despising your enemies with a passion. Intense and volatile feelings would be a sign that splitting is at work. If you become powerfully attached to or fixated upon other people, whether friends or romantic partners—especially if you tend to idealize them—you may rely on excessive splitting. Readers who identified most with **Group 2** statements should pay attention. If you repeatedly become enthusiastic about new people and then suddenly lose interest, you may have trouble accepting the reality of ambivalence in *all* relationships that involve need or dependency.

While we more commonly defend against the awareness of anger, it's also possible to split off our loving feelings when it feels too threatening to acknowledge need and dependency. The chronically angry or dissatisfied person may be warding off more tender feelings; sometimes it feels safer to be self-righteously enraged (such a big emotion!) than vulnerable, hurt and disappointed by someone we love, especially if we greatly depend upon that person.

Emotions

Readers who identify most with **Group 4** statements may occasionally "blow up" or fly off the handle. For long periods of time, you may be successful in *splitting off* your hostile or "negative" emotions, finding outlets for them elsewhere, at a distance; but when you abruptly feel angry at someone near to you, the anger may take over and completely overwhelm you. Sudden, unexpected surges of powerful emotion, especially when it's hard to explain the intensity of those feelings in the moment, often indicate the breakdown of splitting as a defense mechanism.

Sometimes splitting can be a highly stable defense, as in the "even keel" sort of person with a tight rein on her emotions who only occasionally erupts (**Group 3**). Splitting also plays a large role in obsessions and compulsions. In his famous 'Rat Man' case, Freud described a patient with a powerful conflict between loving and hateful feelings; the Rat Man relied on obsessional thinking and compulsive behavior to keep the hatred under control and out of awareness: the obsessions and compulsions keep the split in place, but only through constant vigilance.[16] If you struggle with obsessive thoughts and/or compulsive behaviors, you may be reliant on splitting to keep your aggression at bay.

Splitting as a defense mechanism may also be highly unstable and erratic: some people who rely on splitting shift back and forth between extremes of emotion within a single day. Your views may move rapidly from adoring to despising someone near to you. The problem of ambivalence, how to bear the reality of mixed emotions in all relationships, is a challenge for everyone, especially people who struggle with symptoms of borderline personality disorder.[17]

Self-Esteem

For the person who struggles with issues of shame and low self-esteem, the problem of ambivalence poses an additional challenge. If we struggle for a sense of personal worth, when a loved one frustrates or disappoints us, we often take it as a personal slight that wounds us deeply. We may find it so excruciating that we *hate* them for making us feel that way. We split off our love and take refuge in rage, turning against the person who aroused those painful feelings of shame. Readers who relate most to **Group 6** statements will likely rely on this type of splitting. (I'll have more to say about this specific defense in Chapter Eleven.)

---

[16]Sigmund Freud. *S.E.* **10**, p. 192.

[17]While I see little value in this diagnostic label, the DSM-IV does identify a number of features that often appear together, albeit in nearly all the so-called personality disorders, and in other disorders as well. For our purposes, the most important of these is "a pattern of unstable and intense interpersonal relationships characterized by alternating between extremes of idealization and devaluation." Such alternations reflect the unstable and erratic operations of splitting as a defense mechanism.

EXERCISES

1. What is your political affiliation? If you strongly identify with your party (that is, if you *always* vote for either the Democratic or Republican candidate), review the other party's platform and see if you agree with any of its positions. Politics is one area where people often resort to black-and-white thinking; if you can't find *any* points of sympathy then you may be reliant upon splitting to resolve all ambiguity and nuance, especially if you tend to think in caricatures – i.e., Republicans as gun-toting religious freaks, Democrats as socialistic God haters.

2. Think about one of your early romantic relationships. Can you remember the very first time you felt frustrated, disappointed or angry with your partner? How did you cope with those feelings? Did they raise serious doubts in your mind about whether to continue in the relationship? Did the relationship survive or did the emergence of such challenging emotions bring it to an end?

3. Now consider your current or a more recent love relationship; think about one of your more intense arguments when you felt hurt or let down. How did you express your anger?

   a. Did you explode and attack your partner in hurtful ways (even if you felt they were justified)?

   b. Or at the opposite extreme, were you afraid of anger – yours or your partner's – quickly giving way and accepting blame?

   Both positions reflect the process of splitting: in the first case, you've split off all your good, loving feelings and as a result experience only the hostility; in the second, you've split off your anger because you find it too upsetting or destructive.

4. When you get angry with friends, family or colleagues at work, do you tend to turn away or "write them off"? If you have a

pattern of explosive conflicts leading to a rupture, especially if you tend to feel self-righteous in your own defense, splitting may be at work. Review one of these broken relationships; choose a person whose memory still brings up angry feelings but who once mattered very much to you:

a. Force yourself to consider what happened from the other person's point-of-view. Do not allow yourself to "argue back" or to think *yes, but…*

b. Remember a moment from before the breach when you felt close to the other person; try to recall your good feelings and see if any vestige of them remains. If you can't, then you have successfully split off and denied all the affection you once felt.

c. If you're successful in recovering those good feelings, do you feel any sense of sadness or regret as a result? When we "heal" a split – that is, when we recover split-off love or affection, it often stirs up such feelings of loss, remorse or regret.

d. Or do you feel ashamed instead? Sometimes, we shift from being "completely right" to "all wrong" – another instance of splitting. See if you can come up with a more "nuanced" point of view, where each of you contributed to the misunderstanding.

5. Think back to a period in your life when you went through an extremely difficult time – maybe not as horrific as what my client Chloe had to endure but something truly stressful, full of pain.

a. Did you become more sensitive or "prickly" during this period, as most people do? Did you have less tolerance than usual for the ordinary challenges life throws your way?

b. Did you have any serious disagreements with other people? Did you ever feel "persecuted" by the behavior of a friend, colleague or family member? Did you feel you had enemies?

c. Looking back, can you see how your world view and your understanding of other people were distorted or inaccurate? Do the incidents now seem trivial, compared to how you viewed them then?

Now What?

Building on the preceding chapter exercises, the above exercises encourage you to dig deeper into the role of hostility in your romantic relationships and other intimate connections. So far, we've talked about *denying* and *repressing* anger, *displacing* it and now *splitting* it off and directing it away from a loved one. Managing the potentially destructive force of anger and hatred is a major psychological challenge for everyone.

During the next week, pay attention to any hostile feelings that may arise. Watch how you cope with them, and whether or not you resort to any of the defense mechanisms discussed so far. As I'll describe in Part III, a more effective coping strategy would be to inhibit the first explosive surge of emotion, remembering that all feelings are temporary and will pass in time. Easier said than done!

SEVEN

Idealization

**Sam: I knew it the very first time I touched her.
It was like coming home . . . only to no home I'd ever known.
I was just taking her hand to help her out of a car
and I knew. It was like . . . *magic*.**
– Sleepless in Seattle (1993)

In the last chapter, I discussed splitting as a means to resolve ambiguity, involving either mixed emotions or conflicting attitudes. I also described how splitting often colors the way we perceive people, using the example of wartime, when combatants on the other side of a conflict become very bad and our own soldiers extremely good. As a result of this kind of splitting, we tend to *hate* our enemies and *idealize* our heroes. This chapter looks at the way idealization often accompanies splitting and also functions as a defense mechanism in its own right.

An *ideal* is a standard of perfection, beauty or excellence, and *idealization* means to elevate the ordinary or human to that status of perfection. Most of us have an intuitive grasp of this process; we understand that it involves unrealistic hopes or expectations and often leads to disillusionment, the most familiar example being romantic love. In the beginning of a new romance, the loved one often appears perfect, without flaws or problematic character traits; over time, as this idealization fades, we come to see our romantic partner for who he or she truly is.

If the disillusionment proves too strong, it may bring the new relationship to an end.

In addition to idealizing another person, we may also idealize *an experience* or sometimes *our own selves*.

To idealize an *experience* is to believe it will satisfy us perfectly or solve all our problems: e.g., the person who continually believes everything in her life will be wonderful once *such-and-such* happens.

To idealize *ourselves* is to believe we have no faults or psychological difficulties, or to view ourselves as less troubled or flawed than we actually are. The narcissist, burdened by unconscious feelings of shame about his internal damage (see Chapter Eleven), tries desperately to believe himself perfect and beautiful, envied or admired by others.

I'll discuss these three forms of idealization—of another person, of an experience, or of our selves—in more detail throughout this chapter.

Idealization as a Defense Mechanism

At first, it may not seem obvious that idealization is a defense mechanism. Sure, it's a familiar psychological concept, but how exactly is it a *defense*? In what way does it embody a lie that we tell ourselves in order to ward off pain?

In the same way that splitting *simplifies* the problem of ambiguity—that is, the pain of uncertainty and ambivalence—idealization offers a simple "solution" to difficulties that unconsciously feel hopeless or too painful to confront. That friend of yours who keeps falling in and out of love, who shifts from heady infatuation to bitter disillusionment…have you noticed that he tends to become depressed when each new romance falls apart? You might think that the depression results from disappointment, but in fact, it has been there all along; the failure of idealization as *a defense against depressive feelings* puts him back in touch with those feelings he had hoped to evade.

In other words, some people turn to the drug-like effects of romantic love as a kind of emotional anti-depressant. Their involvement with a relationship partner has little to do with authentic emotional contact or intimacy; what they crave is the "high" that results from falling in love, using it as an escape from pain and depression. The end of a new romance and falling out of love returns them to the feelings they had hoped to cure.

The highs and lows of the serial romantic call to mind the ups and downs commonly associated with bipolar disorder, what we used to call manic-depressive illness (a term I find more descriptive and useful). In fact, manic-depression and serial romance both reflect the flight to an idealized state of mind – infatuation or mania – to escape from unbearably painful feelings.

You may be familiar with the term *hypomania* (literally "below mania") – it's not as extreme and dangerous as the states of mania to be found in manic-depression but similar in nature. Idealized romantic love represents a kind of hypomania whose aim may be to cure unbearable feelings of depression.

Ethan

My client Ethan, an aspiring writer in his mid-20s, suffered from a mild form of manic-depressive illness and was repeatedly falling in and out of love. For days and sometimes weeks at a time, he'd sink into a depressed state so severe he could only just manage to show up for work and make it through the day. At nights and on weekends, he'd shut himself up at home, unable to write or do much more than watch television. Eventually, he'd feel driven out of his apartment to bars and dance clubs, almost consciously in search of a new romance to lift him out of his depression.

When he met a new man, infatuation gave him a kind of "high" that would last until the romance ended ... a few days, a few weeks. Ethan always idealized his partners, endowing them with qualities they did not possess, blinding himself to their actual characters. When reality inevitably broke through, he became disillusioned, broke off the new relationship and sank back into depression. For a long time, Ethan felt unable to face the underlying reasons for his depression – powerful and destructive rage, in part fueled by the expectation that he should have everything he wanted without having to work for it; instead he sought a magical cure in the form of romance, moving from one partner to the next when the drug wore off.

Cultural Images of the Ideal

Maybe you've known people like Ethan, although less extreme in their manic search for love. You might be a serial romantic yourself. Our culture constantly presents us with idealized images of love and "happily ever after," as if the right relationship will solve all our problems; many people look forward to a perfect wedding as the culmination of such love.

Hollywood films, especially within the genre of romantic comedy, bombard us with images of perfect love: incredibly attractive people fall in love, grapple with the obstacles that stand in their way, triumphing over them and eventually riding off into the sunset together – quite literally in that most romantic of films, *The Princess Bride* (1987). That movie is a fairy tale, of course...but then, many adults want to believe in fairy tales.

The search for idealized romantic love involves a longing to attain states of perfection, final solutions to all difficulties, the end of pain and suffering. It reflects the belief in a kind of magic, made clear in the quote from *Sleepless in Seattle* that heads this chapter. When Sam at last takes Annie's hand in the movie's final scene, the viewing audience understands that this touch is magical, too, and the new couple will live happily ever after.

Idealization and Splitting

Idealization in romantic love depends upon the process of splitting: ambivalence about the loved one is "resolved" by splitting off any feelings or doubts that conflict with True Love and then getting rid of them, usually through the process of projection (to be discussed in the next chapter). The serial romantic clings to the illusion of perfection as long as possible, until reality at last breaks through. Then, the partner who formerly had no flaws suddenly has no value. All-good becomes all-bad.

It should be clear by now that such idealized romantic feelings, though we use the word "love" to describe them, bear little resemblance to the kind of love that develops in long-term relationships. Many people talk of being *in love* to distinguish it from other forms of love. Romantic love depends upon idealization of the loved one, whereas more realistic forms of love involve a complex view of the other person, one that often includes his irritating traits, or his behaviors that inspire anger. Idealized romantic love leaves no room for such difficult emotions.

On the other hand, the early idealization that comes with falling in love has its uses. Many years ago, my own therapist told me that such romantic feelings may help us to overcome the anxiety involved in getting close to a stranger. Becoming vulnerable to somebody new, a person largely unknown to us, can be frightening – so frightening that we might avoid the experience entirely and never get close. As a defense mechanism, romantic love (idealization) helps us overcome those fears.

I like to say that a lasting relationship is one where we awaken from the dream of perfect romantic love with someone ideal to discover we're involved with a person who's actually pretty good. Under optimal conditions, as idealization fades, we can develop true intimacy based on a realistic appreciation of our partners. When idealization reflects a more powerful defense and an inability to bear the truth, both internal and external, it instead gives way to disillusionment, despair or depression.

Heroes and Celebrities

In our culture, we also tend to idealize certain public figures, especially famous athletes and movie stars. Rather than seeing them as ordinary human beings like ourselves, we elevate them to the status of perfection: they become heroes who embody our ideals; or as celebrities, they lead enviable lives free of the hardships that govern our own existence.

At first glance, this type of idealization doesn't appear to be a defense mechanism at all. How does idealizing a celebrity involve *a lie we tell ourselves to evade pain*? It's not an extremely powerful defense mechanism, I'll admit, but it does involve a kind of self-deception: some people (we tell ourselves) are lucky enough to lead a life untroubled by ordinary human pain, who don't feel hurt, loss and frustration as we do. Even if they do suffer, it's qualitatively different from our own suf-fering—elevated, even enviable because they are *famous*. In our culture, we worship celebrity as an escape from the ordinary human condition.

Our fascination with the lives of famous movie actors and sports figures may also serve as fodder for shared gossip in small towns, high schools and large corporations. It involves a degree of vicarious fulfill-ment, where we temporarily partake in their more glamorous existence and escape from our own mundane world. On another level, how-ever—usually an unconscious one—we envy celebrities the ideal lives we know will never be ours. For this reason, we take secret (and sometimes not so secret) pleasure in their downfall—hence the tabloid magazines that sell millions of copies with cover stories of betrayal, abuse and ugly divorce.

Idealizing an Experience

People who believe they will finally be happy "if only" something occurs are usually idealizing that future event because they feel unable to address their actual difficulties, sometimes external but more often internal.

My own tendency to idealize certain experiences was (and can still be) quite strong. As a child, togetherness in my family was an infrequent and unhappy experience; the only vacations we ever took were three-day weekends to camp in the Sequoia National Forest or mind-numbing drives from California to visit my mother's family in Texas.

After I had my own children, I would look forward to our family vacations with absurdly idealized expectations, as if this particular trip was going to make everything all right – the perfect family vacation that would make up for my childhood. In the photos from these vacations, you can see my mood begin to sink with the realization that we were still the same prickly, bickering bunch. To this day, my children laugh at me for my idealized fantasy about the perfect family vacation.

Many people idealize vacations in similar ways. Everything will be great once I get to Hawaii. Or – *This place is fantastic! If only I lived here full-time, I'd be happy.* Unfortunately, vacations come to an end; they turn out not to be the perfect antidote to unhappiness after all, and we eventually return to our flawed lives and internal difficulties. The list of possible idealized experiences, often projected into the imaginary future, is endless, of course. Everything will be great once I (a) have a different job; (b) move to a different city; (c) buy that flat-screen TV, etc. *ad infinitem.*

As with romantic love, this kind of idealization often involves feelings of excitement that may function as an emotional anti-depressant. Heightened enthusiasm about the impending event helps us ward off other, more painful feelings; we don't need to confront any immediate difficulties we may have, internal or external, because they *will not exist* once the event comes to pass.

Idealizing Ourselves

When shame and despair about our internal damage are profound, we may feel so hopeless that we deny the truth and create an ideal self-image as a kind of disguise—a fantasy belief in who we are. *I'm not filled with shame and despair about what a mess I am; I'm actually a superior person who other people admire.* This, in a nutshell, is the narcissistic defense. It begins with denial and thrives on idealization. The narcissist idealizes himself and wants other people to idealize him, too.

You likely know someone who behaves this way—who often talks about this *incredible* thing she just did, her *amazing* vacation, how *impressed* everyone was with her at the party she attended, how *lucky* she was to have met so-and-so, the award she received, her incredible evaluation at her last performance review, and so forth. On occasion, you may have felt envious of this person, which is the way she (unconsciously) intends you to feel. I'll have more to say about this dynamic in the next chapter (Projection).

Narcissists depend upon the admiration and envy of others to support their own self-idealization. As narcissism is the primary defense against shame, I'll discuss this kind of idealization of oneself in greater detail in Chapter Eleven.

What to Look For

The search for a complete and permanent solution to complex problems, internal or external, is the hallmark of idealization. Because it usually goes hand-in-hand with splitting, shifts between good and bad (perfection and worthlessness) as well as love and hatred will also be present.

Need and Dependency

People who rely heavily on idealization as a defense mechanism have a difficult time accepting the reality of dependent relationships, where frustration and disappointment are inevitable. When those feelings occur, the person may shift from idealizing someone to devaluing or even hating her.

If you regularly go through such cycles—becoming infatuated with new people (friends as well as romantic partners) and then feeling deeply disillusioned with them so that your relationship no longer has much value—then you may be using idealization as a defense. Readers who identified most with **Group 2** statements may rely upon this defense.

Men and women who idealize others often want to achieve a sort of perfect closeness with another person, at times almost merging identities. You may have known couples who seem "joined at the hip," doing everything together, sharing all the same interests, etc. Maybe you neglect your other relationships when you fall in love, devoting yourself to someone who has become the new center of your universe. Investing everything in one relationship—wanting to be together at all times, as if nothing else matters, and believing that one person holds the key to your personal happiness—is a form of idealization.

People with impossible standards for friends and romantic partners also use idealization as a defense, often because they can't bear the frustration and disappointment that goes along with real relationships. In such cases, they idealize the unmet friend, the future soul mate who will perfectly match their expectations. Unlike real people, the imaginary friend or love object never lets you down, never wants something different from what you want, never behaves in careless ways that hurt you.

Emotions

Manic-depressive cycles, where someone shifts between states of hyper-optimism and despair, involve both splitting and idealization. Even if you don't fit the criteria for bipolar disorder per se, you may still go back and forth between being feeling "just great" and "like shit." If you've wondered before why you seem to be on top of the world one week—full of enthusiasm about your life and future—but down in the dumps a week or so later, for no reason you can easily identify, idealization may be at work. Readers who identify with **Group 4** statements would be prone to rely on idealization.

If you develop many strong enthusiasms that never seem to last – about a new hobby or career, the possibility of living in a different city or country, buying the latest iPhone – idealization may be at work, especially if the ensuing degree of disappointment is equally intense. If you often find yourself thinking something like *Everything could be great if only such-and-such would happen,* then you have idealized that future event.

People who abuse certain types of drugs like cocaine or crystal meth may idealize the high they experience while under the influence, regarding it as the antidote to insoluble personal problems or unbearable pain. People who can't bear their own pain often self-medicate with a wide variety of "drugs," from the endorphin high that results from extreme exercise, to the adrenaline rush of the thrill-seeker. Certain states of mind are idealized and pursued as a "cure" for the inner troubles that can't be faced.

Men and women who demonstrate all the qualities described in this section will have a hard time forming real friendships or sustaining intimacy because the drive toward states of "perfection" leads them away from their own inner truth, thus making genuine contact with others unlikely.

Self-Esteem

When someone unconsciously struggles with feelings of shame, he or she may seek to elicit admiration from others as a substitute for genuine self-esteem. If that struggle is profound, the drive to appear ideal and enviable will be intense. Readers who identified most with **Group 5** statements will likely idealize themselves, making continual efforts to appear as if they "have it all." If you have strong feelings of superiority in relation to your friends or acquaintances – it could be about money, intelligence, looks or your career – and continually find subtle ways to demonstrate your superiority—then you rely on idealization of yourself to avoid feelings of shame or low self-esteem.

When two people with such tendencies form a relationship, they often want it to appear ideal to others. The relationship becomes an extension of each partner's self-image, suffused by the same wish to inspire admiration or envy in others. The romance may depend upon mutual idealization, where you support one another's defensive efforts to ward off shame.

Readers who identified most with **Group 6** statements would tend to idealize other people but run themselves down. They may think in extremely black-and-white terms: *other people have these perfect lives but my own is worthless.* If you often wish you were someone else—if you have idols or heroes who you feel are far, far above you, aristocrats living on some rarefied plane while you are but a lowly peasant—then idealization is at work. How this state of mind, extremely painful in itself, serves as a psychological defense to ward off pain will be discussed in Chapter Eleven.

If you're obsessed with the glamorous lives of celebrities, you almost certainly have a tendency to idealize. Living vicariously through the experience of rock stars, actors and other media figures represents the rejection of your own pain-ridden self and an escape into an idealized realm without suffering.

EXERCISES

1. Think back to a time when you were newly in love or infatuated; try to recall and describe that experience in as much detail as possible. Because this is a common experience, we'll be using it as the paradigm for all idealized states of mind.

   • Did you feel "on top of the world," as if you could handle anything? Did things that had bothered you before suddenly matter less?

- Did you feel incredibly lucky? Did you believe that other people would want to be in your shoes if they knew how wonderful it felt?

Push the writer in you to describe with as much evocative detail exactly how you felt. These heady feelings characterize the state of mind that ensues when idealization is at work.

2. Have you ever formed an intense new friendship that turned sour after a time and ended badly? Maybe at first you felt preoccupied with this relationship in ways that aren't so different from what happens in a new romance. Do you remember the moment or moments when you began to look at the person in a different light? Or maybe it was the feeling that your friend had begun to think less of you, to find fault with your behavior or express irritation over things he or she formerly didn't mind.

- Write a description of the way you first viewed your friend. Even if you despise that person now, take yourself back in time and craft a portrait that would confirm your early feelings. If anything, push yourself to exaggerate his or her good qualities as you describe them.

- Now write down the way you feel about him or her now. As with the prior description, strive for an intensity of expression that really conveys how you feel.

In the last chapter, I discussed how splitting leads to black-and-white views of the world; this particular exercise should help you recognize how idealization may blind you first to someone's flaws and then (once it turns to devaluation) to their good qualities.

3. Think about a time in your life when you were looking forward to an experience with sky-high expectations but felt deeply disappointed when it came to pass. This may have been due to circumstances outside of your control, but it might also have

resulted from idealized expectations. If possible, try to recall an experience when your expectations clearly were the problem.

- Describe how you imagined that experience would unfold before it actually happened. Dwell on the sources of happiness and fulfillment. What exactly was it that you were after?

- Now write down what actually happened and how you felt about it. Try to draw contrasts. You might want to list them in columns, one labeled "Expectations" and the other "Reality."

- Is there any way in which your hopes and expectations clouded your judgment, so that you made choices that, in retrospect, weren't so wise?

4. Do you ever find yourself name-dropping? Maybe you happen to know someone wealthy or spotted a celebrity on the street, a person who your friends and acquaintance would look up to.

- Do you feel that knowing or having made contact with that person raised your status or increased your value?

- Did you secretly hope your friends would feel envious of you or wish it could have been them who had the encounter instead of you?

It might be difficult to admit that you actually felt this way; try not to judge yourself. If these memories stir up feelings of embarrassment about your own behavior, it may be that you were trying to escape from feelings of shame by idealizing yourself, and wanting others to idealize you, too.

5. In a similar vein, in what ways do you try to present yourself to family and friends in an idealized light, exaggerating or over-emphasizing all the good parts and leaving out the bad? Think of an instance where you had an important announcement to make to your family or very good news to relate to friends.

- Did you feel that you wouldn't be accepted or valued unless you presented yourself in such a light?

- How did they respond to your news? Were they happy for you? Did you notice anyone feeling envious? Did anyone try to "burst your bubble"?

- Now reverse the situation: imagine a time when you were in the audience and someone else had news to impart that made that person's life appear ideal to you. How did you feel? Happy for them? Envious? Sad?

6. Think back to another romantic relationship, the early days, when you felt eager to show off your partner to family and friends. Were there ways in which you tried to present yourself in an idealized light?

- In retrospect, do you think that you wanted everyone to see you as incredibly lucky, as having a more attractive/desirable/charismatic partner than any of *them*?

- If you're in a relationship or marriage now, do you make frequent mental distinctions concerning the value of that relationship in comparison to other couples?

- Do you ever see either your own relationship or that of other people as being perfect or close to it?

Now What?

This chapter should have increased your awareness of the way idealization plays an important role in the lives of many men and women, and quite possibly your own. Going forward, pay attention to the way some people describe their experience and try to make it seem ideal. Examine your own hopes and expectations for romance to discern the degree of idealization at work. Pay attention to the painful feelings of disappointment that come up when an ideal lets you down. Those feelings may not be the *result* of disappointment but rather the *reason* you are searching for something ideal.

As a result of the first two exercises, you may also have recognized that the way you feel at one particular moment—say, infatuated with a person you have idealized—isn't always a reliable guide to the truth. While one goal of this book is to help you get in touch with feelings you may have repressed or denied, another is to teach a healthy skepticism about some of your other emotions. As I'll discuss in greater detail in Part III, you don't always have to believe what you feel.

EIGHT

Projection

You're just projecting!
– Said by almost everyone

Projection is another concept that has entered the culture and is widely understood, even by people who've never had any kind of psychotherapy. "Oh, stop projecting," a friend might say. What is usually meant is that you're criticizing another person for doing something wrong when *you*, in fact, are the responsible party. Our expression, *The pot calling the kettle black*, neatly captures this idea.

But projection is a much broader phenomenon; everyone projects to some degree, and the common usage of the term today understates its complexity. To enlarge our understanding, I'll begin with a different way of looking at projection: viewing it as a primitive type of communication – the earliest form of communication, in fact, between parent and child. Instead of *projection*, think about *evacuation* – getting rid of something that feels bad.

How Babies Communicate

Think about the following expressions:

To vent your feelings
To dump or unload on someone
To let off steam

These phrases all imply a kind of evacuation or emptying. Through impassioned speech ('venting" or "letting off steam"), we may relieve emotional pressure; when we complain at great length to a friend ("dumping" or "unloading") we transfer the burden of our feelings onto the other person. The wish to rid themselves of painful emotions, to shift them onto someone else, is what motivates people who make a habit of venting or dumping. They are *projecting* (that is, getting rid of something) in a larger sense than we typically use the term.

Without the benefit of words, infants do something similar, ridding themselves of painful emotion by screaming or crying it out. In the process, this evacuated (projected) pain makes their caretakers feel distressed. Just as you may have felt awful after an evening spent listening to a friend vent, the parents absorb the child's pain and feel highly uncomfortable – so much so that they usually feel the need to *do* something. We feel an infant's pain and try to figure out what it means. Do we need to feed the baby? Change its diaper? Comfort it?

So in an entirely appropriate way, babies evacuate or *project* their unbearable experience into us,[18] evoking an empathic response so we'll help them with their pain or discomfort. From an evolutionary perspective, you could say that projection came into being not only as the earliest defense mechanism, meant to help the struggling human infant cope with (get rid of) unbearable experience, but also as a form of communication that stimulates care-giving responses in the parents. Projection is a normal, everyday part of parent-child relationships and an intermittent feature of most other relationships as well.

In the normal course of things, when they're tended well enough or they're not too difficult for their parents to bear, babies learn to understand and tolerate their own experience. Over the years as they grow up, children don't need constantly to project their experiences outside but

---

[18]While most people usually say "project *onto*," psychodynamic theorists prefer "project *into*" because it captures the unconscious belief that the projected thought or emotion ends up inside another person.

can keep them inside and deal with those feelings themselves. In other words, with the help of its caretakers, the infant's *unbearable* fear, pain, anxiety, etc. gradually become *tolerable*.

It's very much like other more practical parts of child-rearing: after a while, kids learn to use a knife and fork, dress themselves, tie their own shoes, and so forth, so we don't have to do it for them. They learn how to bear their own emotional experience, too, so we don't continually have to help them bear what they feel.

Projection as a Part of Everyday Life

That's an ideal, of course. None of us is completely self-contained and we never entirely give up projecting. Here's another complex example of everyday projection, one that I'm sure will strike a chord with many of you.

Sometimes when I'm extremely tired and worn down, I become irritable with my loved ones. Maybe I'll get snappish or critical, lashing out at people for the *incredibly annoying* things they're doing. Without consciously intending to do so, I will make the people around me feel miserable because I'm such a grouch.

Here's what's happening: I've got an unpleasant feeling that's hard for me to bear alone. It takes a fairly self-aware person to recognize fatigue or grouchiness and simply think, *I got a bad night's sleep*, or *I overdid it this week and I'm feeling pretty thin. It has nothing to do with anyone else.* Instead, I project my experience into those people in my immediate vicinity, causing them to feel *bad* as a result of the way I treat them. Although my snappishness doesn't completely rid me of my unpleasant experience, there's often a kind of relief (usually followed by guilt) that comes from projecting in this way.

You occasionally see a similar process in the workplace. "The boss is in a terrible mood this morning," someone might say to a colleague. "Steer clear!" People in positions of authority may abuse their employees, finding partial relief from their personal suffering by inflicting it on (projecting it into) those beneath them within the corporate structure. In order to put myself through graduate school, I used to work as a litigation paralegal and regularly saw stressed lawyers, on the eve of trial, make their associates and secretaries miserable with their abusive behavior.

Shit travels downstream, the saying goes.

We can understand this as a type of projection, where bad feelings get handed down from person to person within a hierarchy. It's a psychological defense mechanism, meant to rid ourselves of pain. As ineffective and frequently destructive as this type of defense may be, it's important to remember that the person behaving this way is suffering; she feels overwhelmed by her pain and tries to get rid of it by projecting it into others. On an unconscious level, there must also be a hope that someone will understand our cries of pain and do something to help, even if we're no longer babies with parents to take care of us.

In Chapter Five, I described the person who "takes out" his feelings on a friend or loved one when somebody else is the real object of that emotion—an example of displacement. We also take out our feelings on other people when, in an effort to rid ourselves of our own misery, we unconsciously try to make them feel *bad.* At one time or another, most of us have taken out our feelings on those we care about. Under stress, when our more adult coping mechanisms are overwhelmed by the emotional challenges life sends our way, we revert to the earliest form of defense—projection.

I think it's the (sometimes unwanted) role of our loved ones to bear our experience for us when we can't do it alone. Taking on that burden (the projections) is part of loving and caring for other people. Often, when we recognize that someone is projecting in this way, we understand and try to comfort him or her. If we're unable to bear those projections for our own reasons, however—if we're too stressed ourselves or harboring resentments about some other issue—we may instead feel attacked. We may retaliate – try to give the bad feeling back – which can result in an escalating war of projections.

Projection of Guilt

Now that we understand the broader phenomenon that is projection, let's take another look at our more familiar use of the term, where a sense of guilt or a bad conscience is disowned and assigned to somebody else.

Say Jim forgets to do something he has promised to do on the way home from work. When he walks into the house that evening, his wife Stephanie asks, "Where's the dry cleaning?" Jim sheepishly admits he forgot all about it and apologizes. Because Jim has a habit of "forgetting" to do such things, his wife sighs with disgust. "I suppose I'll just have to go pick it up myself tomorrow. Like I didn't already have enough to do!"

Jim suddenly feels defensive, turning on Stephanie in anger. "I don't see why you're making a federal case out of it. So I forgot – what's the big deal? You're always so *judgmental*."

Ever had an exchange like that with a family member, spouse or friend? I certainly have.

At first, Jim admits responsibility and apologizes. Most people can acknowledge guilt under such circumstances, but *only* if their apology is immediately accepted without reservations and they are completely exonerated. Any lingering criticism or harshness makes the experience of guilt unbearable; in that case, many people will reject all sense of responsibility and get rid of their guilt (bad conscience) by projecting it outside.

In this example, Jim's guilty conscience ends up inside of Stephanie, who criticizes him; he then fights her off by turning tables, making her the bad guy. Jim no longer feels guilty about his own thoughtlessness; instead, he tries to make Stephanie feel bad for being such a harsh and judgmental person. On some level, Jim knows that he bears responsibility; the projection involves a "lie" that he tells himself because he can't bear the guilt: *you're the bad person, not me.*

Projection in Romantic Love

Another place to see this process at work is in romantic love. We've all known someone who has fallen in love and we wonder, "What does she see in him?" Or, "Is he blind?" The person in love, often craving the drug-like feelings associated with infatuation, wants to avoid awareness of any inconvenient personality traits in the loved one that might deflate the feelings of infatuation, the delusion of perfect love. So the awareness of faults and flaws is split off; it often winds up in (is projected into) friends or family, who then have to carry all the doubts.

The infatuated person may then avoid or even turn against those people so that he or she won't have to confront the split-off perceptions. Maybe you've had an experience similar to mine, where you felt obligated, out of concern for a friend, to reveal something unpleasant about his new girlfriend, only to have him turn on you. If someone is lying to himself and doesn't want to face the truth, your attempts to open his eyes may feel very *bad* to that person, even hostile, and you can easily become an enemy.

Projection as an Aspect of Character

The above examples involve the projection of one unbearable feeling or hated truth into someone else. The use of projection may also become more pervasive and stable, so that the person's entire character is defined by it.

Here's a classic example. Perhaps you've known a very calm, cerebral, almost detached sort of man. He might be an engineer, lawyer, accountant or some kind of scientist, someone with an analytical mind and his emotional life severely under control. I've known a number of men like this and they often end up married to extremely emotional and needy women. From my experience, it's a familiar dynamic: the one partner gets rid of a large slice of his emotional life and *projects* it into the other partner, who carries it for him.

*I'm not needy, **you** are. I don't experience a lot of painful and scary feelings, **you** do.*

This happens outside of awareness, of course; that is, it's unconscious. The process of projection is entrenched in the man's character, supported by his marriage to a woman who carries all the disowned emotions he can't bear to feel.

Splitting and Projection Together

In Chapter Six, I discussed the problem of ambivalence and the ways we use splitting to simplify or resolve our conflicting emotions. We split them apart and often try to get rid of one of them. As psychological defense mechanisms, splitting and projection often work together as a means to cope with the problem of ambivalence.

Let's say that I have a hard time bearing my anger and aggressive feelings; maybe they were unacceptable in my family of origin and I was expected to be "nice." In truth, I'm a nice and also a *not-so-nice* person, with a mixture of loving and hostile impulses. When the hostility can't be tolerated, however, I will split it off: the loving and socially acceptable feelings – those are *me* – and the hostile aggressive ones are *not me*. Thus I have split myself into parts and disowned one of them, which often means *projecting it* outside.

In Chapter Five, I discussed my client Nicole, a young woman who wept in pity for the wounded bird being tortured by her cruel classmates. Her compassionate, incredibly kind persona was a *reaction formation* to highly sadistic feelings she couldn't acknowledge; at the same time, she *projected* those feelings into the other children, who then came to embody them. Those children actually were behaving in a cruel fashion, so you might say that they *validated* her projection. In my profession, we sometimes refer to this as "projecting into reality."

In the example of forgetful Jim and his wife, Jim has projected his own bad conscience into Stephanie. In his view, she now embodies harsh judgment, making a federal case out of a trivial infraction. But maybe Stephanie actually *is* a harsh and judgmental person; when Jim projects his bad conscience into his wife, she then responds in ways that seem to confirm that the projection has "worked." Entrenched difficulties in many marriages depend upon such a dynamic.

*Why do you always make **me** the heavy?*

You're always doing this–you break your promise, and if I'm angry about it, I'm just this nagging bitch.

Oh stop projecting! Why can't you admit you feel bad for what you did?

Have you ever been around someone who keeps asking you if you're angry about something when you don't at all feel that way? He might ask that question so many times that you eventually do begin to feel angry. It may be that he's onto something you don't realize, but it could also be that he has projected his own anger into you and now perceives it to be there, identified with you, rather than inside himself. The persistent questions–"Now are you absolutely positive you're not mad at me?"–may eventually provoke the very feeling that has been projected, as an (unconscious) sort of confirmation that the defense has succeeded.

In other words, when people rely upon projection as a defense, they often try to validate the projection–that is, convince themselves it has succeeded–by saying or doing things that will evoke the disowned experience in other people.

Projection and Anxiety

Sometimes when people project or evacuate an emotional experience they're unable to bear, it might not take such a distinct personal form but instead may be felt as a kind of nameless dread or fear of some imminent threat from the outside. In working with people who suffer from anxiety disorders, I've often found that their anxiety signals a fear that the projected emotions will return and overwhelm them. This can feel terrifying, all the more so because they don't understand what they're afraid of.

Theresa, one of my clients, resembled Nicole in many respects: shy and soft-spoken, her personality seemed void of all aggression, although she excelled at the almost-imperceptible put-down that sounded nice on the surface. Like so many of my clients, she came from a highly chaotic background. Her family led an almost nomadic life; her mother was emotionally unstable and her father remote. As a result, Theresa never felt safe in the world. As she grew older, she became almost agoraphobic and suffered intense panic attacks.

As we worked together, we came to understand that she had projected a huge part of her emotional life because she found it unbearable. On an unconscious level, she found her own hostility so threatening that she feared she might fall apart if she were to "own" it. Instead, she projected it into the ether, so to speak. The outside world came to feel more and more threatening, which caused her to lead an ever narrower life in order to avoid coming into contact with what she had projected. Sometimes, even ensconced in the safety of her home, those feelings would threaten to become conscious, resulting in a panic attack.

This type of anxiety, where projected and disowned hostility threatens to return, may also produce efforts to curtail and control it through obsessive types of thought or compulsive behaviors. I'll discuss such defenses in Chapter Nine.

Projection and Shame

In the section about idealization of oneself from the last chapter, I described a person who finds ways during your conversation to mention, for example: how much money he earns (it's a lot more than you do), or the name of someone important he knows (but you don't); this amazing and incredibly expensive vacation he just took (which you could never afford); how impressed so-and-so was with him; the new car he just bought; the glamorous party he attended last week, and so on.

You probably dislike this person. You may think of him as snobby or ostentatious. Whenever you have contact, he leaves you feeling unhappy, with a bad taste in your mouth.

People who idealize themselves and flaunt their superiority also want to make you feel badly about yourself – in fact, that's the very point of their behavior. Sometimes, it's deliberate but more often, it's an unconscious attempt to undermine your self-esteem and make you feel inferior. The person who wants so much to seem like a winner needs a loser over whom to triumph. Sometimes these people fill you with envy, too, and you want to tear them down afterwards – mock or belittle them to anyone who will listen. Sometimes hatred isn't too strong a word for the feeling they inspire.

The character Helen in the film *Bridesmaids* (2011) perfectly exemplifies these traits. A beautiful socialite, married to a wealthy man, she makes constant references to the important people she knows, amazing places she's visited, her intimate knowledge of the best restaurants in town, the top designers, the best places to shop, best venues for a bridal shower – the best, in fact, of everything. In particular, she flaunts her superiority to rival Annie, the maid of honor, whose life is hitting bottom.

Annie hates Helen. She hates her because Helen consistently makes her feel like a complete loser. At the end of the film, once Annie has redeemed herself and escaped the pit of self-loathing into which she had fallen, Helen finally admits that she has no friends and that nobody wants to spend time with her, not even her husband. On the surface, she appears to be a winner, but in fact, her social life and marriage are barren. She feels like a loser herself – exactly the way she tried to make Annie feel.

What Helen projects—what those ostentatious, self-aggrandizing people try to project—are feelings of inferiority. They unconsciously try to undermine your self-esteem, to fill you with envy, to demonstrate your complete inferiority so that they can feel superior and above you. These individuals are often hyper-competitive: for them, the world is composed of two (and only two) types of people: winners and losers, yoked to one another as polar opposites.

They defend against the conviction that they belong among the losers by projecting that feeling into you and trying to make you feel it.

You are the loser and I, in contrast, am the winner!

What to Look For

Projection as a facet of human psychology plays such a large role, appearing in so many different guises and defending against virtually every painful emotion that this chapter serves only as an introduction to a very large topic. Here are some of the many ways that projection might show up.

Need and Dependency

I find it helpful to think of emotional needs and vulnerabilities as the "baby parts" of ourselves; we express our more adult or parental aspects when we function responsibly in the world and take care of ourselves, looking after our needs or finding the appropriate person to meet them. In other words, we're a mixture of parent and child parts; either aspect may be projected into other people.

Men and women who can't bear to feel needy will sometimes develop relationships with highly dependent friends and partners, assuming a "Rock of Gibraltar" role or becoming a "tower of strength." The person who never seems to need anything and whom others lean upon as a kind of parent has undoubtedly defended against the awareness of his or her own needs.

He may have *denied* his needs and *repressed* all knowledge of them; at the same time, he may *project* them into other people who must then carry them for him. Readers who identified most with **Group 1** and **Group 3** statements would tend to rely on this type of projection.

In contrast, other people may project their adult or parental side into someone else and try to make that other person responsible for all caretaking. You may have known someone whose life is always falling apart and needs to be rescued by his parents or friends. *Look at what a mess I've made of things – you have to take care of me because I'm clearly an incompetent child!* Readers who identify most with **Group 2** and **Group 4** statements would likely project in this way.

As you might imagine, the Rock of Gibraltar and helpless "child" often attract and complement one another, forming highly stable but unhealthy relationships.

You might see similar dynamics in families or the workplace: between parents and their adult children, among co-workers or colleagues and in friendships. Look for lop-sided or asymmetrical relationships, where one person seems much needier or dependent than another. Fully mature relationships involve reciprocity, where each party depends upon the other to have needs met, and in turn, satisfies the other person's needs as well.

Emotions

When we project (disown) a feeling we can't bear, we often find someone else to carry it for us, as in the example of forgetful Jim who made his wife into his guilty conscience. At other times, the projection may be more violent and explosive: maybe you know someone who blows up under pressure and makes everyone around him miserable. It might help to think of such a person, whatever his age, as a baby overwhelmed with pain, screaming in order to rid himself of that experience.

If you've been around someone who behaves that way, you know how uncomfortable it feels; you may find the person's company unpleasant, stressful or even offensive. If you tend to rid yourself of unbearable feeling in this way, other people may try to avoid you. Maybe you feel you're "too much" for your friends and family, and it might in part be because you rely upon this type of projection. Readers who identified with **Group 4** statements should pay attention.

If people around you often get angry with you for no reason you can understand, you may be projecting your anger. If you often "guilt" people, you may be avoiding a painful sense of responsibility for something you don't want to face. Readers who respond most to **Group 3** statements would likely project in this way.

Self-Esteem

Marked feelings of superiority, contempt and smugness, along with the attitudes of condescension and self-complacency usually signal that shame has been projected into other people. So do a competitive sense of being more attractive, successful, popular, etc. Readers who identify with **Group 5** statements will project in this way.

These and other defenses against the awareness of shame will be discussed in greater detail in Chapter Eleven.

EXERCISES

1. Examine one of your close relationships and consider how need and dependency play a part. It could be with a friend, family member or romantic partner, but preferably *not* a minor child or physically disabled parent. If possible, think of a relationship where one of you is considerably more needy or dependent than the other, or where one of you does a disproportionate share of the giving.

   • Is there some external reason why this is so, or is it a function of your personalities?

- If you're the needier one, how do you feel about being in that position? How does the other person treat or respond to you when you're in a place of need?

- If the other person is the needier one, how do you feel about him or her when this disparity becomes obvious? Does it bother you that you give so much and receive comparatively little in return?

- Take some action that purposefully reverses these roles. For instance, if you tend to be the needy one, do something extremely generous in which you take complete charge and the other person is passive. Ask for nothing in return.

- Or if you're the Rock of Gibraltar type, ask your friend or partner to do something for you where you will be completely dependent on that person to get your needs met. Don't just ask for help, as in the exercise from Chapter Four; to the extent possible, make yourself helpless.

- Take note of your feelings and be on the look-out for discomfort. This exercise should stir up strong feeling as you step out of your comfort zone and challenge your defenses.

2. The second exercise is designed for people who struggle with anxiety or suffer from panic attacks. It will also be useful for individuals who worry that something bad will happen if they're not extremely careful—i.e., with a tendency toward obsessive thoughts or compulsive behavior.

- What exactly is it that you're afraid of? You may have come to dread the pain of your anxiety, but try to look beyond it. Does your anxiety have a focus, some particular experience that you're determined to avoid?

- Can you imagine a scenario in which your worst nightmare comes to pass? Write it down in great detail. Beyond anxiety, is there some other emotion you're afraid to feel?

- It's likely that your anxiety level will start to rise as you continue writing the disaster scenario. As this occurs, try shifting into a different fantasy: envision yourself engaged in some aggressive activity. It could be battling a mythical dragon or punching the face of someone who hurt you. Try working up some anger within the fantasy.

- Can you forge an emotional link between anxiety and anger? Do those two emotions connect for you in any way?

3. Try to recall an argument where you felt defensive, as if the other person was trying to make you feel guilty. It would help if you still feel some heat about the incident.

   - Do you feel a strong urge to defend yourself and make the other person into the heavy? Do you feel as if you're arguing with him or her in your thoughts?

   - Looking back on the incident, can you shed your defensive feelings for a moment and find a place where you might actually have been at fault, at least in part? Do you feel any guilt or shame about it?

   - If so, write out a statement which explains exactly what you did that was hurtful, insensitive or mistaken; don't make reference to the other person's contribution, only your own behavior.

   - If you're still in contact with this person, try having an actual conversation where you take responsibility for what you did but say nothing about what you feel the other person did or should have done.

   - Take careful note of how you feel and how the roles may shift. Does the other person then own his or her part or instead continue trying to make you feel guilty?

Now What?

The exercises in this chapter encourage you to challenge your accustomed roles and step out of typical behaviors. In Part III, when we discuss in greater detail how to disarm your defenses, I'll be stressing the importance of this type of effort for challenging those defenses that are embedded in your personality. The defensive aspects of our own character may be difficult for us to see, so central are they to our identity.

For now, pay attention to the following pairs and see whether your relationships divide up in these non-reciprocal ways:

Rock of Gibraltar - Helpless Child

Even Keel – Emotional Roller-Coaster

Always in the Right – Always Screwing Up

Don't look only for extremes; these roles may play out in subtle ways that might take a little study to detect.

As I discussed earlier, when we rid ourselves of (project) some aspect of our experience – feelings of need, strong emotion or a sense of shame – we often find someone to "carry" it for us. Begin now to examine your relationships for ways in which you may each project something into one another.

NINE

Control

I'm an ordinary man, who desires nothing more
than an ordinary chance to live exactly as he likes,
and do precisely what he wants.

– from *My Fair Lady* (1956)

Superstitions

The well-known behaviorist B.F. Skinner once conducted a series of experiments using hungry pigeons in a cage attached to a mechanism that automatically delivered food at regular intervals, without reference to what the birds were doing beforehand. Skinner found that the pigeons would associate the delivery of the food with whatever they happened to be doing at the time it was delivered, and that they continued to perform those same actions, often bizarre and ritualized, as if there were a causal relationship between those actions and the delivery of the food. In other words, the pigeons came to believe they could influence the arrival of food with their behavior.

Skinner considered these actions analogous to human superstitions such as rituals for changing one's fortune at cards. In tribal cultures, this type of superstition is quite common; many pantheistic religions use ritualistic behavior such as animal sacrifice in an effort to influence divine action. In modern America, professional baseball players commonly use superstitious rituals when going up to bat. Superstition is everywhere.

Many people believe they will incur bad luck if they open an umbrella indoors, walk under a ladder or cross paths with a black cat, so they avoid those actions in order to evade misfortune. Ancients once believed that a sneeze caused the soul to escape from the body through the nose, and that uttering the appropriate words would prevent the Devil from seizing it. To this day, many of us still say "Bless you" when somebody sneezes.

Have you ever crossed your fingers and told your friends to wish you luck, just before you started to do something that mattered deeply to you? As if your fingers and the wishes of your friends had any effect on the outcome!

Superstitions represent the longing to master an unpredictable world, to feel we have some control over what happens to us when in fact we're often quite helpless. It might console us or boost our confidence if we believe that crossing two fingers will bring good fortune, but in truth it has no more causal effect on external events than the weird behavior of Skinner's pigeons on the timing of their food's delivery.

Helplessness and Control

The experience of helplessness is painful and difficult; making efforts to gain control over our circumstances in order to mitigate such helplessness is a natural response. In the states along Tornado Alley, people typically build storm cellars; the citizens of California often have earthquake preparedness kits in their homes; in Louisiana, the Army Corps of Engineers maintains dikes to control flooding. We do what we can to control our unpredictable environment, but in truth, we're more vulnerable than we like to admit.

Most of us have a hard time living with the constant awareness of that fact. You can't go through every minute of your life conscious that you're not in control, unable to predict what will come next. It's one of the reasons why we fall into routines, why we take such comfort in repeating certain traditions. Routine and tradition help us feel that we have some ability to predict what's coming next. Living an orderly life provides some solace in the face of an erratic, uncontrollable universe.

Think of order, tradition and routine as healthy defense mechanisms – small "lies" we tell ourselves to ward off existential anxiety in a largely unpredictable world. Taken to an extreme, however, these defense mechanisms create their own problems.

Many people fall into routines so immutable and lifeless that they strip their experience of emotional vitality.

The so-called "neat freak" deals with his anxiety by exerting massive control over his environment, often driving people around him to distraction in the process.

The person who strives for control through compulsive rituals often feels tormented by them.

Sometimes, it is the very unpredictability of our feelings that we find hard to bear – why we feel them, what instigates them and how long they will last. In Chapter Two, I talked about my client Sharon who used bingeing-and-purging as a way to rid herself of emotion in a ritualized, highly controlled fashion. Over the years, I've also worked with several women who self-injure: although the psychological issues in self-injury are complex, all of these women used cutting as a way to exert control over their pain.

If I cut myself right now, and in this location, I am able to dictate when it will happen and how it will make me feel. It will go on as long as I want it to.

Like all defense mechanisms, control may help us to manage unbearable emotions, but when it becomes too extreme or deeply entrenched, it creates an entirely new set of problems.

Dependency and Control

Whenever we enter into a relationship with someone else, that person begins to matter to us and as a result can influence the ways we feel. Once I fall in love with you, I endow you with the enormous power to wound me. If you become my friend, you can hurt my feelings with your indifference or insensitive behavior. Even relationships at work, such as the one between you and your boss, have the power to inspire deeply painful emotions beyond your control.

One reason people get married is to gain a basic sense of predictability and control in the face of scary feelings like jealousy or a fear of abandonment. Given the high divorce rate and increasing impermanence of marriage in the modern world, you might argue that the sense of predictability is an illusion, but most people still seem to crave it. Other factors, emotional and biologic, influence the urge to marry, of course, but the desire for a sense of permanent connection in the face of uncertainty plays a major role.

The wish to believe you can count on another person – a spouse, friend or co-worker – is natural. Taken to an extreme, however, the desire to be *absolutely certain* leads to behavior we commonly refer to as *controlling* or *possessive*.

The jealous man who needs to know each and every detail of his partner's schedule.

The micro-manager at work who tries to regulate what every one of her employees does on the job.

The friend who wants to take possession of you, to know everything about your life and be included in all you do.

In other words, when our need or desire for other people makes us feel unbearably helpless, we may attempt to control them. You might remember Brian, the client I mentioned in Chapter Two, who married a submissive woman and secretly installed surveillance equipment to monitor her behavior. At least he wanted contact and entered into a relationship, as controlling and possessive as he turned out to be. Other people find such vulnerability intolerable, especially if their earliest encounter with dependency–during infancy and early childhood–taught them it was unsafe to be so vulnerable. In order to avoid that experience, they may entirely shun intimate relationships, living in isolation.

Stealth Control

While we've all known domineering people who actively seek to control others around them, there are other, less recognizable types of control. In particular, some men and women seek to control their partners through the very fact of their own helplessness. While they may appear extremely needy and incapable, they often have an unacknowledged fantasy of controlling their partners; they may unconsciously believe that, through their helpless behavior, they are *forcing* the other person to assume the role of caretaker and that they can manipulate the partner into giving what is wanted, be it emotional or financial support.

In other words, the person who appears extremely needy and helpless often has no more tolerance for actual dependency than the person who tries to control other people; they're both defending against the awareness of dependency but in different ways, one via active control, the other through an invisible effort to manipulate and thereby gain control. Men and women who appear helpless and almost infantile may unconsciously believe they hold all the strings, controlling the people around them as if they were puppets.

The cultural stereotype here is of the helpless female, but it doesn't always work that way. Early in my training, I had a client, a young man I'll call Terry, who suffered from severe depression and had a history of relationships with older men who would financially care for him. I was working at a low-fee counseling center at the time; even with our sliding scale, Terry found it hard to pay for his sessions and tried to manipulate me, using my fear and anxiety for his welfare when he became anorexic into giving him treatment for free.

When he lost his job and told me he could no longer pay, I was on the verge of agreeing to see him several times per week at no charge when my supervisor helped me understand the dynamic of control between my client and me. When I informed Terry he would nonetheless have to pay the clinic's minimum fee ($5 per session), he eventually became enraged that he couldn't make me look after him. I learned a lot from working with this client, especially about the anger and fear of *genuine* dependency that lies behind such manipulative forms of helplessness.

I stood my ground. Terry found another job and lost it; over time, he learned to hold one down and take care of himself.

In our daily lives, many of us enact the same sort of drama on a smaller scale:

Do you "forget" to do things around the house, chores you may have promised your partner to do, in the secret (probably unacknowledged) hope that somebody else will do them for you? This same dynamic sometimes lies behind procrastination, the hope that you can get somebody else to do the job if you put it off long enough.

Do you ignore looming financial difficulties, for so long that by the time you're paying attention, you have to ask your parents to bail you out?

The male who can't seem to keep his apartment clean often harbors a fantasy that Mommy will always be there to pick up after him, if only he can coerce her into doing so by waiting her out. (I'm *not* talking about the guy who really doesn't care if he lives in a pigsty; I've also known messy women who unconsciously wished for someone to clean up after them.)

Look behind the apparent role of helplessness and you'll usually find an intolerance of real need and stealth fantasies of coercive control.

Self-Esteem and Control

Whenever someone becomes important to us, he or she gains the ability to influence how we feel about ourselves as well. If a person I value and respect turns around and rejects me, it will wound my self-esteem no matter how self-confident I may feel in general. Although human relationships strengthen us in certain ways, they also increase our vulnerability and cede to others the power to influence how we feel about ourselves.

Because we're social animals and necessarily express our personalities in relation to other people, even casual acquaintances and strangers may have an effect on how we feel about ourselves. If you went out on a first date and found your interest in a second date wasn't reciprocal, it would hurt to some extent. If you were telling a favorite story to someone you'd just met at a dinner party and the other person made it clear he found you less than interesting, it would wound your self-esteem.

To a degree, we all try to regulate how other people view us. *Putting your best foot forward* means to present yourself in ways that accentuate all your strengths. Rather than leaving it to chance, we attempt to control the other person's impression of us by highlighting our best qualities. *This is how I want you to view me – observe these qualities, in particular.* Especially in situations like job interviews where making a good first impression matters, attempting to have this kind of "control" over another person makes sense.

When making a new acquaintance at a party, most people try to put their best foot forward, as well. *I'll tell you about my successful career and the European vacation I took last summer but probably won't mention that my daughter just dropped out of college and has me worried sick.* Wanting to look your best in front of strangers is understandable, maybe even natural.

Taken to an extreme, wanting to look your best becomes the intense effort to make sure that other people admire and envy you. It may involve so much exaggeration or distortion as to represent a kind of lie. In other words, it is a psychological defense mechanism. *Pay attention to these truly amazing things about me so that you (and I) will never see all the things I can't bear to face about myself.* Defensive efforts to control how you are viewed lie at the heart of narcissism.

I'll return to this particular dynamic in greater detail in Chapter Eleven, *Defenses against Shame.*

What to Look For

Except for the clandestine type of control that masquerades as helplessness, this defense mechanism shows up in distinctive character traits not too difficult to spot. Most of us try to exert control over our experience to some extent—it's only natural—but men and women who rely heavily on control as a psychological defense often get tagged:

She's really bossy.

Why do you have to be such a stickler for detail?

You're so controlling.

Things always have to go exactly his way...or else.

What a neat freak!

Extreme reliance on control often comes to define one's personality.

Need and Dependency

Some people try to make sure they never feel needy or dependent. At an extreme, they may be loners or avoid intimacy entirely. Like Henry Higgins in *My Fair Lady*, vowing that he "will never let a woman in [his] life," they won't let anyone get close enough to matter. They continually disqualify likely prospects, or date someone for a while then break it off just when intimacy threatens to develop.

In order to have complete mastery over his life, the person who relies heavily on control never allows himself to depend upon another person, reserving the right "to live exactly as he likes and do precisely

what he wants." He may affect a kind of indifference to human relationships, vowing never to marry, but he's actually warding off a fear of
helplessness and dependency.

I don't need anyone.

If you believe that you have a "problem with intimacy," the
way we usually describe this issue, it may be that you fear the loss of
control that would come were you to let someone else matter emotionally. You're afraid that making yourself vulnerable reduces your ability
to predict the ways that you will feel. In an extreme form, this defense
may lead to estrangement from friends and family members, as well. If
nobody matters, then nobody has the power to hurt you. Readers who
identified most with statements from **Group 1** and **Group 3** may rely
upon this defense.

At the opposite extreme, some people form new attachments
quickly and soon want to exert control over the other person. With
unusual self-awareness, an acquaintance of mine once told me, "I don't
make friends, I take hostages." You may have known someone like this
who wanted to be your best friend soon after meeting you. These people
can become possessive and jealous of your other friends. At some level,
they want to own you.

This dynamic often shows up in family relationships where there
are separation issues. Parents who find it hard to let their children grow
up can't bear the feelings that arise as they separate: the loss of closeness,
the longing for contact when the child desires to move away, the feeling
that you no longer matter in the ways you once did. In order to avoid
such painful feelings, parents may try to control their children and prevent them from separating.

Possessiveness in romantic relationships shows up when the person has a difficult time bearing separateness. It may feel so threatening to be dependent and vulnerable that we try to assume control over
the other person. If you're a jealous, possessive person, you most likely
have a hard time needing other people because it makes you feel unbear-

ably vulnerable, out of control. When you're apart and you have no idea what your partner is doing, you may feel deeply anxious. In order to manage the feeling, you will strive to exert some control over your partner (**Group 2**).

If your life seems like a series of emotional upsets and you frequently need help managing them, if important people in your life often feel the need to take care of you, they may be responding to your efforts to elicit help. Unconsciously, you might be using your "helplessness" in order to control other people, forcing them to come to the rescue. On a lesser scale, if you often forget to do things you've promised to do and others around you have to pick up the slack, of if you put off confronting problems until someone else has to step in, you may be unconsciously controlling the people around you, forcing them to cope on your behalf.

Emotions

People who rely heavily upon control to manage their emotions may appear extremely even-tempered or possibly detached. They may reduce their lives to a highly structured regimen with virtually no variation, in order to believe they can know exactly what they will feel and when. If you're deeply wedded to your routines and dislike change, if you're easily upset by unanticipated events, you likely rely on control in order to minimize unexpected emotion in your life. This would apply to readers who identified with **Group 3** statements.

Compulsive behaviors might be thought of as highly ritualized routines and serve the same purpose, to exert control over an unmanageable emotion and the attendant feelings of helplessness. The anxiety surrounding the compulsion signals an underlying terror that your experience will get out of control, that intense emotions will flood and overwhelm you. The nature of those unconscious feelings will vary, but the compulsive person always fears that those feelings will be unbearable if they break into awareness. The feared result would be total disintegration – captured in our everyday language.

When I heard the news, I just went to pieces.

If you have compulsive behaviors that feel out of your conscious control, you're likely terrified that some unconscious feeling will break free of the control you're exerting through that compulsion.

Self-Esteem

Wanting to put one's best foot forward is natural; continually striving to regulate how people view you is a different matter entirely. If you devote a lot of energy to the impression you make, devising ways to influence or impress people, then you rely upon control, most likely to ward off feelings of shame, both conscious and unconscious. Readers who identified most with statements in **Group 5** will almost certainly resort to this type of control.

The self-deprecating individual exerts control in the opposite way. The self-inflicted put-down so often seems to elicit, even to *demand* a contradiction: *That's not true! You look wonderful in that outfit!* You've probably said something similar, wondering if the person had only criticized his or her appearance in order to elicit your compliment. Sometimes that's the conscious intent but more often the effort to control your response is unconscious. These people crave praise and acknowledgement so much that they can't bear to sit by and wait for it to come.

And sometimes the deeply shame-ridden person puts herself down in order to prevent anyone else from doing it, announcing, in so many words: *You can't tell me I'm a loser because I already pointed it out myself.* As hard as it may be to believe he's not trying to manipulate you, to get you to contradict him, he's actually trying to exert control over an anticipated experience that would devastate him. He may hate himself, and speak of himself in degrading ways, but it feels better than hearing contempt from the lips of someone else. Readers who identified with **Group 6** statements would likely resort to this type of control.

EXERCISES

1. Are you superstitious? Think it over and don't answer too quickly. You might occasionally have said something like *I'm afraid to talk about it as a sure thing because then it won't happen.* Maybe you have a lucky number when you buy lottery tickets. Do you consider yourself a lucky or unlucky person? If so, what do you think influences or determines this kind of luck?

2. Take a look at your life and assess the importance of routine. Are you a creature of habit?

   • Does it upset you when your routine is disrupted?

   • When you make plans, do you have a hard time adjusting to it when those plans are changed at the last minute?

3. If other people describe you as a neat freak, even if you don't feel yourself to be one, take a few days and stop straightening up. Leave some dishes in the sink overnight; drape your clothes on the back of a chair rather than hanging them up. Don't make the bed. Take careful note of your reactions and describe the ways you feel. Hold off the major tidying effort as long as you can.

4. If you're the sort of person who naturally takes charge, to whom family members normally look to make decisions, try taking a back seat for a week or so. If the others ask you to make a choice for them, decline to do it. If you're the type who, in contrast, always looks to others for guidance, try stepping up to the plate, if only for a few days. Force yourself to be more decisive even if you're not entirely certain about the best course of action. In both cases, watch carefully for the ways this unaccustomed behavior will make you uneasy. Pay special attention to any change in the ways you may feel about yourself and the other people involved.

5. Think of an experience that made you feel completely helpless. Try to recall exactly how you felt and describe it in as much detail as possible. If you can't come up with anything, then imagine yourself in a situation where you'd feel frightened and out of control. Write out the scenario. Be vivid.

   • How did you (or would you) find comfort in the face of helplessness?

   • What is it that helps you to feel less out of control?

6. Examine the role of control in your relationships with friends, family and partners.

   • Who wields the most control and how do they exercise it? The bossy person will be easiest to identify, but see if you can identify any kinds of passive behavior, in yourself or others, that represents a kind of stealth control.

   • If you're married or in a romantic relationship, does one of you have more control over your sex life than the other? Does one person tend to decide when and how often sex takes place?

   • If so, try reversing the roles. If you have more control, try letting your partner set the terms. If you tend to be passive, consider being more assertive in initiating sex.

Now What?

As in the last chapter, the exercises here encourage you to challenge your typical roles and step out of your comfort zone. Recognizing a defense mechanism at work won't lead to change by itself; you need to put insight to work and choose to behave differently if you're to grow. I'll discuss the importance of choice at greater length in Chapter Thirteen.

For now, you can begin by taking a close look at routine in your life and exploring how you feel when you step out of it. Begin in small ways: if you eat the same thing for breakfast every day, try something different. If you watch the same TV programs each week, go out to a movie, read a book or take a walk instead. Avoid doing the familiar things that feel most comfortable and confront the unknown. Pay attention to the new ways you feel.

Then take a bigger step and do something entirely out of character, something that makes you feel vulnerable and out of control (not dangerous, of course). As a young man, going out to eat alone or to a movie by myself stirred up a lot of anxiety. Find something analogous for you and be brave. Making change and choosing to do something different takes courage.

TEN

"Thinking"

Michael: I don't know anyone who could get through
the day without two or three juicy rationalizations.
They're more important than sex.

— *The Big Chill* (1983)

To some degree, the majority of us carry on conversations with ourselves "in our heads," more like a running monologue in many ways, and we refer to it as *thinking*. For most people, this flow of mind-words occupies a central place in their awareness of themselves as a sentient being.

I think, therefore I am, said Descartes: my sense of self arises, in part, from the words streaming through my mind.

Thinking seems like a constructive process, and of course it is; without thinking, human beings couldn't respond creatively to their world, make discoveries, come up with new inventions, etc. Thinking enables us to take steps in our imaginations first, before taking them in reality, often saving us from grave errors. A great deal of sage advice recommends the interposition of thought before action.

Look before you leap.

Think before you speak.

Act in haste and repent at leisure.

All these sayings convey the idea that thought, as an imaginary form of action, can save us from pain and regret. Thinking is perhaps the most valuable tool in the human repertoire.

On the other hand, thinking sometimes feels as if it "turns against" us and becomes a nuisance, even a kind of torment. Have you ever found yourself unable to fall asleep because you couldn't switch your mind off? Have you ever felt obsessed with something—a fight you had with a friend, or an important career decision to be made—and found you couldn't *stop* thinking about it even when you wanted to? Thinking is a very powerful instrument, but sometimes, to go *on and on* thinking feels like torture.

And if thinking often embodies a kind of internal dialog, a running commentary we make to ourselves, then the question also arises: what if the things we tell ourselves *aren't actually true*? Sometimes thought becomes a kind of internal lie, leading us away from ugly truth or covering up a painful reality; in those cases, we're employing thought as a psychological defense mechanism.

This chapter looks at the two main examples of thinking as such a defense—rationalization and intellectualization—concluding with a look at how the process of thinking overall may embody a type of psychological defense.

Rationalization

Stop kidding yourself!
Oh come on, get real!
You're only lying to yourself.

These are but a few of the many expressions we use when we believe another person to be self-deceived. He may have told us something, made a statement explaining what he believes to be the reality of a situation, and we feel certain that he has talked himself into such a view, largely because he *wants* to believe it rather than because it really is true. *Wishful thinking*, we might call it. We infer a mental process of self-deception, one that involves verbal thought in the service of a lie.

Sometimes the lie being told involves the *justification* of some feeling, motive or action, trying to make it seem acceptable or valid – in other words, making excuses when we actually feel uneasy about it at some level.

It's okay that I downloaded a pirated copy of that CD because I'm a poor student and those greedy record companies have so much money it won't make any difference to them anyway.

We also make excuses for our actions – that is, we rationalize them – when we don't want to accept full responsibility for what we've done.

The reason I got such a lousy grade on that paper is that the teacher doesn't like me (and not because I didn't work hard enough on it).

We might also come up with logical reasons to explain something we've done, making it seem entirely rational, when in fact we were driven by feelings we don't care to admit, not even to ourselves.

I went out and bought that new outfit because I really had nothing to wear to Jane's party (not because I knew the ex who dumped me would be there and I wanted to look especially good and happy, as if I didn't feel the least bit humiliated).

As Michael notes in the quote from *The Big Chill* that heads this chapter, we all rationalize our feelings and actions; it's part of everyday life and we'd have a hard time getting through it without a certain amount of self-deception. *Things will work out for the best,* people often tell themselves, warding off feelings of loss or regret. *Everything happens for a reason,* we say, when in truth, life is largely unpredictable and random. Rationalizations help us to feel we live in an orderly world that evolves according to some larger plan when it's actually a random universe where painful things often happen to us for no good reason.

Bolstering our self-esteem is another area where rationalization plays an important role in our daily lives. *Diane got that promotion instead of me because she's ruthlessly ambitious and has the boss fooled.* Doesn't it feel much better to believe such a story than to accept that

Diane is simply more gifted at the job than you are? *Brandy likes David more than me because he's got a lot of money and a nice car.* Maybe she just finds David more interesting and attractive, period.

For the most part, this type of rationalization is not an especially powerful defense; the truth often lies not far beneath the surface, and with a little help—when someone confronts us with the truth in a way that doesn't feel critical or accusatory—we may acknowledge it after a brief struggle.

Intellectualization

While rationalization as a defense mechanism offers explanations for *specific facts* that are more plausible than true, intellectualization seeks to keep *the entire spectrum of disturbing emotion* at bay. The former might be thought of as the occasional *white lie* we tell ourselves, the latter an ongoing system that embodies a big ongoing lie: *no disturbing emotion here, only dispassionate thought.* Rationalization is a discrete, occasional defense, whereas intellectualization pervades and defines one's entire character.

Sigmund Freud never used the word intellectualization, although he clearly understood that the intellectual process may be used for purposes of defense. His daughter Anna Freud devoted an entire chapter of her book *The Ego and the Mechanisms of Defence* to the subject of "Intellectualization at Puberty." She believed that the "increased intellectual, scientific, and philosophical interests of the period represent attempts at mastering the drives and the connected emotions," viewing such an effort as relatively normal during adolescence.[19]

If you grew up with the late 1960s TV series *Star Trek* as I did, or if you've made acquaintance with it through televised repeats, movie sequels or DVDs, then you're familiar with the character of Mr. Spock, the half-

---

[19]Anna Freud. *The Ego and the Mechanisms of Defence* (1936); (London: Karnac Books, 1993), p. 172.

Vulcan who consciously feels little emotion and brings a powerful intellect to bear on every situation, in contrast to Captain Kirk who so often seems driven by his passions. Better than perhaps any other character in popular culture, Mr. Spock demonstrates intellectualization and how it comes to define one's entire character.

You sometimes hear such people described as cerebral; or we might talk about someone who lives too much "in his head." I find it useful to think about intellectualization in terms of our *attention* and where we direct it. The person who intellectualizes her experience devotes so much attention to the thoughts passing through her head that she doesn't have room to notice what's going on in her body.

Taking note of bodily sensations helps us to recognize what we're feeling. A welling up of tears, tightness in my chest and quivery breath — these sensations let me know that I feel sad. But if I'm too busy with my thoughts, I may not be able to notice those sensations and will thus remain unaware of emotion. Even if I do register some kind of sadness, I may quickly shift my attention away from the bodily sensations into my thoughts, in order to get away from them.

In other words, intellectualization is a massive and ongoing effort to divert attention away from the bodily places where we notice our feelings and into the emotion-free zone of the intellect.

Precocity

Individuals who rely heavily on intellectualization are often those people who wanted to grow up quickly, because early family life made them feel it was unsafe to be small, needy and at the mercy of their emotions. While not always the case, precocious children may take flight into a kind of pseudo-maturity in order to escape the experience of being small, developing an intellectual self out of touch with their emotional experience. If the parents are high-achievers who expect their offspring to fulfill their own idealized expectations, those children may feel as if there's no room for them to be small, with the normal fears and emotional vagaries that are part of growing up.

As adults, such precocious individuals may feel as if they're imposters. Dreams of showing up for class unprepared to take an exam or appearing naked in a social situation reveal the unconscious fear that their intellectual sophistication is but a sham. Despite great verbal fluency and an impressive ability to manipulate concepts, they feel as if they have grown up only "on the outside," with a vulnerable child or baby hiding behind the façade.

Many years ago, a client brought me a succinct dream image depicting intellectualization and what it may defend against. In her dream, she saw a standing figure in a white lab coat with a mortarboard on his head, sporting large black glasses (they reminded her of the ones worn by the cartoon scientist Mr. Peabody of the Wayback Machine). Underneath the lab coat, he was wearing diapers. Thus a detached, scientific intellect may offer an escape route from the scary "baby" feelings below.

You probably know someone with a highly intellectualized way of viewing the world, a Mr. Spock sort of person who rarely feels passionately about anything and who strives to be objective at all times. On an unconscious level, these individuals are terrified of their unpredictable, uncontrollable feelings, taking flight from them into the emotion-free realm of thought.

The Overall Process of Thinking as a Defense

In the case of pseudo-maturity, the child escapes into precocious intellectual development in a way that reflects a kind of denial: *I am not small, helpless and inexperienced; I'm actually quite knowledgeable and advanced.* In such cases, intellectual and verbal ability develop prematurely, but detached from authentic experience and as a *defense against it.* Words take on a life of their own and are often felt to have an almost magical ability to ward off or defuse pain.

In my family of origin, according to lore, when I began to speak I started talking in complete sentences—no baby talk, no faltering attempts to master language. During treatment, my therapist suggested this was my way of expressing a hatred of feeling small and inexperienced; I wanted to sound grown up right away without going through that lengthy process of actually maturing. My precocious command of language also reflected a reaction to my mother's depressive illness, felt to be invasive and overwhelming: by mastering words and language, I felt in control. I believed that "thinking" helped me escape from unbearable pain and confusion (hers as well as mine).

As a result, I have always over-valued verbal fluency, living too much in my head where I am carried along by the mental flow of words. Going through school, I wrote papers that *sounded* sophisticated; I had a facility with concepts and could manipulate them in persuasive ways, but the realm of words and ideas existed in many ways apart from my personal experience, out of contact with and in denial of it. A big part of my journey as a writer and as a client in therapy was to reconnect those two realms.

Many of my clients over the years have come into treatment with similar defenses. I can usually recognize this process at work when I'm listening to someone who speaks with apparent insight into her experience, but leaves me feeling disconnected, at a distance. For these individuals, "understanding"—the entire realm of verbal thought—may function apart from true meaning and serves to ward it off, especially the most painful parts. You might think of it as a kind of internal sophistry, where we continually deceive ourselves with specious ideas and arguments meant to hide the truth.

Verbal thought sometimes takes on a life of its own, in perpetual defense against unbearable emotions, becoming a kind of torment. So many clients I've known have talked about the agony of being unable to sleep because their minds won't quit. I believe this dynamic lies behind many types of insomnia. As is often the case with powerful defense mechanisms, what begins as a means to protect ourselves evolves into a problem in its own right: pain isn't the problem as much as what we do to defend against it.

The degree of the underlying pain does explain why silencing the verbal defense and establishing mental quiet is so incredibly difficult for most people: as with all defenses, letting go means opening up to pain, finding out what you've been avoiding all these years. With rationalization, that means challenging those little white lies you sometimes tell yourself; with intellectualization and the use of verbal thought as a defense, it involves the more daunting task of reviewing your entire character structure and the ways you have functioned throughout your life, learning to think a lot less in order to feel more.

What to Look For

Rationalizations are fairly easy to spot ; but because they're pervasive, built into our character structure, intellectualization and "thinking" are harder to identify.

Need and Dependency

A rationalization often occurs at the moment when a person trying to lose weight breaks one of the rules for his diet.

It was the day from hell at work and I deserve some ice cream tonight – just a small bowl. I can always make up for it tomorrow.

*I'm feeling way too deprived, and if I go on like this, I'll blow my diet in a major way. A little break will actually **help** me stick to my diet.*

Everyone knows how hard it is to need or want something – to be conscious of desire – and yet be unable able to satisfy it. Even if we're eager to lose weight, hunger can feel unbearable. We rationalize violating our long-term goals in order to gratify our immediate desires; that is, we lie to ourselves in order to get what we want *right now*. Readers who identify most with **Group 2** statements may use rationalization in this way.

Men and women who struggle with various addictions often lie to themselves, and to other people around them, in just this way. Alcoholics are notoriously dishonest, with themselves and with their loved ones; they rely primarily on denial but also use rationalization in order to evade awareness of the damage that results from their drinking. *I'm not hurting anyone but myself* is a common lie that alcoholics tell themselves and other people.

They also try to minimize the severity of their problem and make it seem "normal."

Everyone has a vice. No one is perfect.

What a stressful day! This drink will help me get through my next meeting.

It'll help me relax and get to sleep so I can function better tomorrow.

In general, rationalizations tend to come up when our long-term goals or values conflict with the wish for immediate gratification. We attempt to evade the pain of deprivation with a lie about the true nature of our motives or the actual consequences of our actions. If you frequently make excuses for your substance abuse, for those instances when you go off diets or fail to follow through on goals you've set, you likely make use of rationalization.

In contrast, rationalizations also come up when we can't have what we want. Aesop's fable of the fox and the grapes illustrates this process. *They're probably not even ripe anyway.* This type of rationalization represents a lie we tell ourselves to ward off unbearable desire, envy or regret. The woman with perfectly good reasons why she *does not care* about some disappointment is using rationalization to explain away the sense of loss. The man who logically tells you why he *would never want* to be in the (objectively enviable) shoes of a friend has rationalized away his envy. If you related most strongly to **Group 1** statements, you may use rationalization in this way.

People who unconsciously fear intimacy may have a very logical explanation for why they avoid it. They rationalize the urge to run away from emotional dependency, disguising their fear with plausible reasons.

I can't get involved until I figure out what I want to do with my life.

It makes sense to date casually right now, until I'm ready to settle down. I don't want to lead anyone on.

Men and women engaged in careers that involve a great deal of analytic thought may become so deeply engaged, even passionate about their academic research, their legal briefs, their chemical or quantitative analysis that they have no room left over for emotional relationships. They may convince themselves that success in their career demands a kind of single-minded focus that makes relationships difficult, if not impossible.

People who rely on "thinking" and intellectualization as their primary defense mechanisms may live so entirely in their heads that they have little contact with their bodies, where need and desire are noticed. They may seem very "dry" (a client once described these people as having "no juice"); they may come across as cerebral and even asexual. On an unconscious level, they likely find need and sexual desire terrifying. If you have little interest in sex and no desire for human contact, living primarily in your head, then intellectualization is one of your primary defenses.

Intellectualization might feature strongly in the personalities of readers relating most to **Group 3** statements.

Emotions

Rationalization often gives us an excuse not to follow through on commitments, or to express hostile feelings we don't consciously acknowledge. In this area, it may be a favored defense of readers who identified most with **Group 4** statements.

If it were me and I thought someone was coming to dinner at my house only because he'd promised, I'd rather he stay home unless he really wanted to come. I'm just going to cancel, even if it is at the last minute.

*She might feel I'm being cruel but it would be much crueler **not** to tell the truth. Honesty is the best policy*

Or that parental favorite: *It's for your own good.*

Sometimes honesty really is the best policy, and parents often do things for the benefit of their children that feel unfair to their offspring, but sometimes these rationalizations simply mask the genuine motive or feeling. In regard to the above three examples, the person might actually (unconsciously) feel:

*I don't care if I promised. John called and I'd much rather see **him** tonight.*

I really want to get back at her for what she said the other day.

I'm tired of dealing with you and I resent all this deprivation. Parenthood never lets up!

Rationalizations keep us from having to acknowledge the so-called negative emotions: anger and hatred, envy, jealousy, resentment, selfishness, etc. Instead, we write those feelings out of our personal stories and substitute a rational explanation for our behavior. Sometimes you can spot this type of rationalization because you tend to keep repeating it with a vague feeling of mistrust or guilt; you may feel the need continually to justify yourself. I'll talk more about this feature of many defense mechanisms in Part III.

Intellectualization tends to ward off the whole spectrum of human emotion and is readily identified as a prominent personality feature, as I discussed in the prior section. This person fears strong emotion and will tend to avoid situations or involvement that will stimulate it. The cold, distant or detached person fears the heat of strong feeling. "Thinking", on the other hand, might be more noticeable at certain times than others. In my own case, when I'm particularly stressed or upset, my thoughts take off. It's my way of trying to cope with an experience that feels like "too much." If I'm not careful, it means I won't sleep much that night.

Sound familiar?

Whenever the chatter picks up speed and swells in volume, it's an indication that some painful feeling is threatening to overwhelm you and you're trying to ward it off.

Self-Esteem

Rationalization may be useful when we've said or done something that stirs up shame. Reasoning away "guilt" is something we all do.

I did her a favor—in the end, she'll thank me.

He really had it coming.

After all, I had a perfect right to speak up—there's absolutely no reason I should feel bad.

As described in the prior section, we tend to repeat our rationalizations in order to shore up the defense. If you hear yourself explaining, again and again, why you shouldn't feel ashamed or guilty, take heed.

Where intellectualization functions as a defense against shame, brilliance of thought may be valued as a kind of superiority, felt to invalidate the underlying (unconscious) feelings of shame. The person who believes himself to be much smarter than and therefore superior to everyone else often comes across as arrogant or condescending (think of the Mark Zuckerberg character in *The Social Network*). He has taken refuge in his brilliance, bolstering this defense by looking down on other people; he may become especially heated during intellectual debates and feel driven to prove those lesser minds "wrong."

As I'll discuss in the next chapter, the person who defends against shame often tries to make someone else feel the shame instead; if you often feel contemptuous of or impatient with other people and continually rub them the wrong way, if you have a powerful need to win every debate, then your intellect may be functioning as a defense against unconscious shame. Readers who identified most with **Group 5** statements should pay attention.

EXERCISES

1. Set aside half an hour and pay attention to your internal thought process. In other words, take note of what you are thinking as you think it. The goal here is merely to become a conscious self-observer.

   - Are your thoughts primarily verbal? To what degree does your thinking resemble a kind of internal monologue?

   - Do you feel as if you have control over the mental flow of words? Can you start and stop it when you want, or focus it wherever you'd like?

   - Now strive for mental quiet – that is, see whether you can silence the thought words. Shift your attention into your body, to the places where you might register emotion: face, belly, throat, torso.

   - How long can you last before the thoughts start up again? Did you notice any specific bodily sensations during the silence? Were they uncomfortable?

2. On a day when you don't have many commitments, undertake a short fast – say skip a meal or two without snacks. Allow yourself nothing but water or juice then watch carefully as hunger begins to mount. Do you try to rationalize breaking the fast? Do you make perfectly reasonable excuses for yourself to eat?

3. If you believe you have an addiction of some kind – it could be substance abuse or sexual behavior – try holding off longer than you normally do before gratifying yourself.

- If you can hold off long enough, it should give you some insight into the experience you're trying to avoid with the addictive behavior.

- It might also reveal the ways you mentally justify your habit. Listen carefully to your thought process, the words running through your head; do you make excuses for yourself or come up with entirely plausible reasons why you should go ahead and give in?

4. When something happens that bothers you and you find yourself thinking the incident over and over again, try to stop the mental flow of words. See how long you can last. In contrast to the way I've asked you to make use of other exercises:

- *Don't* try to describe what you're experiencing.

- *Don't* write anything down.

- *Don't* try to understand or make sense of what you feel.

- Simply pay attention and take *non-verbal* note of your experience. Don't be dismayed if you find this task extremely difficult.

5. Try to recall a time when you expressed a strong feeling or lashed out at someone and kept trying to justify your behavior afterwards.

- Write down a thorough and logical explanation for your behavior. Push yourself to an extreme and come up with as many justifications as you can.

- Now imagine someone arguing the opposite point of view, explaining why each of your reasons is invalid. Do you feel defensive?

- Assume for the moment that there really is no valid justification; how do you feel?

6. Do you place a high value on your intelligence or take special pride in being especially articulate?

- How do you feel about people less intelligent or articulate than you are?

- Do you remember any times when you came across as inarticulate or unable to think clearly in the heat of the moment? How did you feel as a result of that experience?

- Have you ever deliberately tried to make someone look foolish or stupid because the person held an opinion that differed from your own? In as much detail as possible, describe your feelings for that person and his or her views.

- Now try to put yourself in that person's shoes. Exercise your imagination and try to *feel into* that person's experience, making his emotions your own.

- If you can feel his sense of shame or humiliation, it might help you understand the feelings you're trying to ward off.

Now What?

In my experience, most of us rely to a degree on the defense mechanisms discussed in this chapter. Because the process of thought is at the core of individual consciousness, it's crucial to develop some skepticism about our own thinking if we're to detect the lies we tell ourselves. The exercises in this chapter should help you become attuned to this process, at the same time encouraging you to re-focus attention away from your head and into your body. In Part III, I'll discuss the process of "locating" our feelings in greater detail.

While you might do the same with all the exercises in this middle part, you need to work especially hard to generalize this experience, making it a part of your daily life. We rely upon our thought processes to justify *all* of the defenses we use, as a kind of back-up or second-ary defense. For this reason, tuning into those thoughts and questioning their validity is the starting point for disarming our defenses, which will be discussed in the final part of this book.

ELEVEN

Defenses Against Shame

**A woman ... so ugly on the inside she couldn't go on
living if she couldn't be beautiful on the outside.**
— from the film *Seven* (1995)

Of all the painful emotions described in this book, a core sense of shame
is the most excruciating, the most difficult to bear. My views on shame
and its origins likely differ from the way you normally think about it,
so before describing the most common defenses against shame, let me
clarify these views with a brief detour into neurobiology and early infantile development.

At birth, we human beings are intensely vulnerable and reliant
upon our mothers and fathers to help us grow. The course of our development depends upon how they respond to our physical and emotional
needs, and we enter this world with a set of inbuilt expectations for what
those responses ought to be. Winnicott referred to this genetic inheri-
tance as a "blueprint for normality."[20] When our parents respond appropriately, in keeping with that blueprint, it feels natural, right and good,
instilling us with a sense of safety in our world and of our own intrinsic
beauty. As discussed in Chapter Three, this experience forms the core
of self-esteem.

---

[20] D.W. Winnicott. The basis for self in body. In *Psycho-Analytic Explorations*, ed. C.
Winnicott, R. Shepherd and M. Davis (London: Karnac, 1989).

But in situations where the parents' responses diverge dramatically from that blueprint—say, when their behavior is emotionally abusive or traumatic—the baby senses that something is *very wrong* and feels unsafe in its world. On a deep intuitive level, it *knows* that its own development has gone awry. Instead of instilling a sense of intrinsic beauty, an abusive or traumatic environment leaves the infant with a sense of internal defect and *ugliness*.

I refer to this core sense of intrinsic defect as basic shame. At heart, the experience of basic shame, often unconscious, feels like inner ugliness, the conviction that if others were truly to "see" us, they'd recoil in scorn or disgust.

At first glance, it might seem as if I'm using the word *shame* in a totally idiosyncratic way, but this usage actually reflects one of the secondary meanings of the word: *disappointed expectations*.

It's a shame the rain spoiled our picnic.

When anticipating the day ahead, we have an idea in mind, a vision of the pleasure we will take in the planned picnic; when the reality fails to match that expectation, we call it a *shame*—in a sense different from but related to the primary meaning of the word. In the case of the developing infant, basic shame arises when the inbuilt expectation for a nurturing environment is disappointed by the reality of parents whose behavior is abusive or traumatic. That experience truly is a shame in the secondary sense, and results in feelings of shame in the primary sense.

Studies by Allan Schore[21] and other experts in neurobiology have traced the effects of parental responses to their infant on the development of the baby's brain, especially those parts involved in feelings and social functioning. In comparing brain scans of two-year-olds who grew up in emotionally deficient environments—that is, with parents who consistently failed to respond according to the infant's inbuilt

[21] Allan N. Schore. *Affect Regulation and the Origin of the Self: The Neurobiology of Emotional Development.* (Mahwah, New Jersey: 1994).

expectations—with those who grew up in optimal environments, the former displayed far fewer neurons, with fewer interconnections between them.

In other words, when the environment diverges widely from the blueprint for normality, failing to provide the emotional responses the infant needs, its brain develops *abnormally*, analogous to the way that a deficiency of Vitamin D (rickets) during childhood may impede normal bone development. After two years, those abnormal brain developments become lasting; you can never fully make up for inadequate parenting during this critical period.

Again as with rickets, where failure to rectify that Vitamin D deficiency will lead to permanent skeletal damage, the brains of babies whose parents consistently let them down emotionally will reflect that damage *for life*, primarily in the areas of self-worth and the capacity to connect emotionally with other people.

Basic shame is the (often unconscious) awareness of this internal defect, felt at the deepest level of our being.

To express these ideas in terms of our primary psychological concerns (Chapter Two): in order to develop normally after birth, we need parents who will tend to our needs, help us learn to manage our emotions in the context of a loving, joyful relationship and make us feel safe in the world. These are the conditions we need in order to thrive, emotionally and neurologically. When our parents fail, we're unable to develop as we normally would; growing up, we *know* on an intuitive, deeply felt level that our development has gone awry, instilling a core sense that *something is wrong with us.*

We don't need a perfect environment upon birth, only one that is "good enough," in Winnicott's terms. As we move along the spectrum of possibilities away from "good enough" toward more limited, traumatic and abusive environments, those defects increasingly impact and damage our development. The sense of basic shame will also intensify along that spectrum: the more deficient the early experience, the more pervasive will be the sense of damage and thus of basic shame. These feelings will be carried by the person throughout his or her life.

Even if the early environment isn't abusive or highly traumatic, we may develop pockets of shame when our parents let us down in important ways. Maybe boundaries between mother and child are confused, and the parent has difficulty bearing separation. A mother may become so mired in anxiety or depression that it limits her ability to meet her baby's needs, etc. In these cases—somewhere between "good enough" and highly deficient—the damage may be less severe and so will our feelings of shame or internal ugliness; our defenses against that experience won't dominate our character so pervasively.

In my experience, a great many people have these pockets of shame.

People who struggle with basic shame typically rely on three common defenses in order to ward off the painful awareness of it: narcissism, blaming and contempt.[22] I came to link these three defenses and connect them to shame because my experience as a therapist taught me that they go hand in hand. *Narcissism* is the primary defense against (unconscious) shame. Many people who struggle with such shame have a hard time acknowledging fault or error and tend to *blame* others instead. They often project their internal "ugliness" and feel *contempt* for it outside, in other people. I'll discuss each of these defenses in turn.

---

[22]You won't find this trio on Anna Freud's list of the most common psychological defense mechanisms, although blaming might be considered a form of denial. (*There's nothing wrong with me; it's you who are at fault.*) Melanie Klein viewed contempt as a type of defense, but against the awareness of need rather than shame. Andrew Morrison (*op. cit.*), building on the work of Heinz Kohut, did write in depth about narcissism as the response to an underlying sense of shame, though he conceives of shame in a way that fundamentally differs from my own views expressed here.

The Primary Defense against Shame

The quote that heads this chapter describes a person who flees from inner ugliness and takes refuge in physical beauty. In Oscar Wilde's famous novel, Dorian Gray's portrait (hidden from public view) reflects his hideous inner self while on the outside he remains physically young and impossibly handsome. The apparently beautiful but deceptive outside thus masks a truly ugly person within: this is the basic narcissistic defense. It's horrible on the inside, but *ideal* on the outside.

While we're more familiar with the type of narcissist who over-values her looks and wants to be admired or desired, it's also possible to idealize one's public persona in order to ward off shame. I gave some examples in Chapter Seven, discussing idealization as a defense. Whether it's about their wealth, success, popularity, sophistication or glamour, many people strive to appear ideal. They seem to be saying *Look at me – I've got it all! Admire me. Envy me.* Somewhere in the attic – or more appropriately, the basement (the unconscious) – there's an ugly, shame-ridden self they don't want you or anyone else to see, ever.

On my website and in my YouTube videos, I often use the film *Avatar* as a metaphor for this flight from shame into an idealized self – a self that is largely fictional or false. Just as Freud employed the myth of Narcissus – a Greek youth who fell in love with his own reflection – in order to illuminate a psychological phenomenon he then named narcissism, I employ *Avatar* as a kind of myth that sheds light on the primary defense against shame.

At the opening of the movie, Jake Sully has suffered a severe spinal cord injury that leaves him a paraplegic. No longer able to perform as a combat marine, Jake volunteers for a specialized military mission to the planet Pandora. There, through the miracle of technology, he learns to psychically link with and inhabit an "avatar" or alternative physical self on that planet.

In contrast to his damaged paraplegic self, this avatar is healthy, fit and stands ten feet tall, with enormous physical prowess and sensory capabilities beyond those of humans. Embodying this avatar allows Jake not only to regain the functions he lost but also to *surpass* his human potential. His experience on Pandora ultimately proves to be more real, more meaningful to him than his actual life; at the movie's end, he finds a way to transcend his physical damage and move permanently to the realm of his superior Na'vi self.

David

Like Jake Sully, my client David longed for a new, superior identity to conceal the damage. A number of years ago, back when chat rooms and bulletin boards were first heating up, he became obsessed with the world of online "relationships." A short, slightly overweight and physically unexceptional man in his mid-30s, David suffered from extremely low self-esteem. His family background was deeply troubled; during his late teens, his mother committed suicide and David dropped out of college not long after her death. He never managed to find and apply himself to any meaningful career and had spent most of his adult life either supported by his father and step-mother or working in low-level retail jobs.

Despite a deep longing for connection, David had never managed to develop a relationship of any duration; instead, he tended to become fixated upon unattainable men, extremely attractive and successful members of the "A Gay" social world, as he called it. Often he developed subservient relationships with these people: he'd try to win their love and affection by "doing" for them. Invariably, they'd take advantage of him, giving rise to feelings of resentment on his part. Eventually there'd be an explosive confrontation that usually ended the friendship. David was a deeply unhappy and lonely man.

When he discovered Internet chat rooms, he found a way to become (at least in fantasy) the person he'd always longed to be. As

I believe is often the case in anonymous online "relationships," he completely misrepresented himself. The online David was younger, taller and thinner than the real one; he had a dynamic career and drove a different car, owned his own home, etc. Online David had it all.

Often these relationships moved from the Internet to the telephone; he took great pleasure in "meeting" these strangers and getting to know them through hours-long phone calls. They'd eventually make plans to get together; he'd re-schedule at the last moment and put off the meeting as long as possible. Eventually he'd either stop returning phone calls and disappear from the other man's life, or make a shamed confession and beg off.

David was burdened with profound and intolerable shame. Because he couldn't face that shame and how he felt about his own damage, he found authentic relationships impossible. Instead, he took flight from ugly, damaged David into attractive and successful Online David. Like Jake Sully, he left his damaged self behind and escaped into an ideal new self.

To a degree, David was conscious of taking flight from himself. The more successfully defended narcissist may have little idea that the self he or she presents to the world is fictional, illusory, a denial of internal damage. David ultimately knew he couldn't keep up the pretense because he had so thoroughly misrepresented himself that a face-to-face encounter would immediately expose the lies. Other narcissists may more successfully deceive themselves as well as other people.

Ordinary vs. Defensive Narcissism

When Freud first began discussing narcissism, he viewed it as a sign of mental illness, a withdrawal of interest in and desire for other people, redirecting those feelings toward oneself; eventually, he came to understand that narcissism is also part of the normal human experience.

It's healthy to be interested in yourself, to hold yourself in high esteem, to feel sure you're a person who others would also value. Ordinary narcissism lies at the heart of self-esteem and self-confidence. When extreme – that is, when it becomes defensive in nature – narcissism shows up instead as arrogance and conceit. Rather than an unspoken, taken-for-granted belief that one is a person of value, defensive narcissism always has something to prove.

Narcissists may feel an ongoing need to demonstrate some kind of superiority. They live in continual relation to a real or imagined audience, a group of spectators who must look on with envy or admiration. Through their behavior and the things they say, narcissists may subtly (and sometimes not so subtly) communicate that you are beneath them. *I'm smarter than you. I earn more money. I know important people you don't. I'm more interesting, more attractive, sexier, more charismatic, etc.*

Because the effort to deny shame and internal damage requires constant support from the outside, narcissists also demand your attention. *Look at me! Listen to me!* You may be more familiar with those narcissists who make physical displays, placing their bodies at center stage and using their looks to evoke desire, but narcissists come in many different varieties:

The social bore who goes on and on talking about himself and has no interest in anyone else.

The extreme extrovert, often quite charming, who dominates conversation with entertaining stories that don't necessarily paint her as superior or desirable. The important point is to remain at center stage.

The artist or athlete who continually puts his talent on display, demanding your approval.

For all narcissists, the goal is to monopolize attention. They demand the interest and admiration of others because they unconsciously feel damaged, ugly and worthless.

The Shame-Driven Superego

People who struggle with shame often *expect* themselves to be ideal, in order to escape from and disprove their sense of inner damage. They demand perfection of themselves and when they fail to meet this standard, they go on the attack.

No doubt you're familiar with the *superego* – Freud's name for the aspect of ourselves that observes, evaluates and criticizes us, the voice of our morals and values. In German, Freud coined a new term for this concept, *Über-ich*, a compound formed from two everyday words; it means something like the "Over Me," because it feels as if we're being watched (and criticized) from above. As usual, the English translators opted for a more scientific-sounding term and came up with *superego*.

This term has now been incorporated into our everyday vocabulary and become part of our shared understanding of human psychology. Most of us understand exactly what someone means by talking about a *harsh superego*. People who struggle with shame often have especially savage (and savagely perfectionistic) superegos. The price for falling short of perfection is an assault of self-hatred so brutal it negates us.

To put it in language closer to the actual experience, we may feel like:

a total fucked up loser

a worthless piece of shit

damaged goods ready for the trash heap.

The return of shame feels excruciating, made all the worse by the self-loathing that comes along with it. For the person with narcissistic defenses, that experience will prove unbearably painful; in order to evade or ward off that pain, they result to additional defense mechanisms.

Blaming

The pairing of shame and blame is extremely common. People who strive to appear ideal and feel threatened by a return of shame find it difficult to hear anything resembling criticism. Because the price for "failure" or imperfection is brutal self-hatred, they will deflect all criticism, shifting the blame onto others.

One of my clients, Holly, relied heavily on this defense, especially in relation to her husband Eric. Following one of their fights (usually occasioned by some hostile and provocative behavior on her part), Holly would spend hours reviewing the argument in a highly accusatory way, going over all of Erik's faults and progressing to total character assassination.

Underneath (unconsciously), she felt ashamed and guilty about the "crazy" way she instigated these fights. In our sessions together, we covered this territory so thoroughly that I developed a shorthand means of pointing it out. I'd sigh in an exaggerated and aggrieved way and say, as if from her point of view, "That Eric!" She found it hard to acknowledge her role in these fights because it filled her with shame and self-loathing.

Holly saw the issue in terms of black and white: either (1) she was entirely right and Eric to blame; or (2) she was such a messed up nutcase that we might as well give up and flush her down the toilet. Like all savage perfectionists, she had a hard time believing in *step-by-step growth* that happens gradually. For a long time, the idea of *learning from experience* meant little to her.

Most people with a harsh or perfectionistic conscience find it difficult to believe that growth may occur bit-by-bit, over time. Like Holly, they avoid admitting failures and find it hard to acknowledge the hurtful ways they behave. For this reason, they find it difficult to learn from their experience, instead engaging again and again in the same self-defeating behavior.

Contempt

Another client, Ian – a therapist-in-training himself – would listen carefully to the comments I made to him and often say, "But how am I to know if what you're saying is true? Maybe you're right; maybe some other way of looking at it is just as valid." On the surface, these remarks appeared neutral; on another level, I felt his complete contempt for me.

Ian had a habit of responding to things I said with his *own* interpretation, delivered in a condescending tone with an almost imperceptible smirk. He sometimes talked to me as if I were stupid. I often appeared in his dreams in some degraded way – in tatters, filthy or disfigured. Rather than feeling his own shame, his sense of internal damage and ugliness, he turned me into a pathetic loser instead.

You might have known someone like Ian who feels superior to everyone around him and is skillful at making you feel like an idiot. For the entrenched narcissist, being ideal usually means feeling *above* other people; it means proving oneself to be a winner and triumphing over the losers. Such narcissists will be extremely competitive. They need continually to prove themselves victorious and therefore better than everyone else. Feelings of smugness, superiority and contempt for others go along with this type of competitiveness.

By triumphing over the other person, the narcissist "proves" that he has successfully rid himself of his unwanted shame. Feeling contempt for and humiliating the loser confirms his idealized self-image. In keeping with earlier chapters, we might also say that the narcissist *denies* his shame and *projects* it into the other person, triumphing over it.

The Defense of Last Resort

When shame utterly dominates the way we experience ourselves – when the damage feels deep and pervasive – the usual defense mechanisms often fail to help us. We may find it impossible to defend against the truth with lies to ease the pain. Like my client David, such individuals may seek refuge in fantasies but never try to realize them. They disappear into books or movies; through vicarious fulfillment, they escape from shame and shed their damaged selves. You might think of it as a concealed form of narcissism.

Individuals with such overwhelming shame usually struggle with powerful self-hatred, as well. They suffer under an image of the perfect, superior self they're supposed to be, cruelly attacking themselves for failing to live up to that ideal. It's as if they can imagine only two possibilities — the inferior, damaged loser they feel themselves to be, and the ideal person they long to become. The beauty or the ugly freak. The enlightened one or the imbecile. They may view the external world in the same terms, with only two categories of people: the winners and the losers.

Although such men and women sometimes seem to be without defenses, mired in shame and self-hatred, their perfectionism embodies a defense of last resort: *while I may be a contemptible loser, at least I know enough to look down upon and despise myself. I'm not such a fool that I actually accept who I am!* The inner voice that belittles and brutalizes them in fact expresses their own contempt — the same kind of contempt, as discussed earlier in this chapter, which serves as a defense against shame.

This may be a difficult concept to grasp. In therapy, my clients will describe how much they suffer from such cruel perfectionism, as if they live under a corrupt and ruthless regime that dominates with brutality; it's a challenge to help them see that the brutal dictator is *also* an aspect of themselves, the part that utterly rejects their damage, demanding perfection instead.

I am a superior, contemptuous god; I utterly despise and reject that fucked up loser!

They refuse to accept that they must make the best of who they are, face their shame and damage, beginning to grow from that base.

Complete self-rejection and self-hatred of a perfectionistic nature is the defense of last resort against shame.

What to Look For

Although this chapter will speak most powerfully to readers who identified with the statements in **Group 5** and **Group 6**, many people struggle with issues of shame irrespective of the defense mechanisms they use. The (often unconscious) knowledge that we've been damaged by our upbringing carries with it feelings of shame, even if our parents or other important people didn't shame or humiliate us during childhood. Virtually every client in my practice has had to grapple with shame at one time or another.

Need and Dependency

Shame-ridden individuals may feel embarrassed by their needs. They may believe there's something humiliating about desire. Because they feel damaged and unworthy, these men and women may find intimacy too hard to manage, or will enter into an abusive relationship with somebody who "confirms" the shame by degrading or devaluing them. Such individuals are often described as having no self-esteem or feelings of self-worth (**Group 6**).

By contrast, the person heavily defended against shame may seek out partners with low self-esteem to carry the shame instead. In other words, the damaged, shame-ridden self is projected into the other person, who then becomes the inferior member of a winner-loser partnership.

What may be less obvious is the way the superior partner carries and expresses the type of self-hatred described in the preceding section. The superior member's contempt may show up around issues of dependency, where she scorns her partner for being weak or needy. Readers who related most to **Group 5** statements would be prone to engage in this type of relationship.

Emotions

For the shame-ridden individual, ordinarily bearable emotions such as envy or jealousy become toxic, though they often show up in disguise. Poisonous envy might appear instead as cloying compliments that don't ring true or repeated self-deprecating comparisons that eventually become annoying to the listener. The envious person might also launch humorous little digs at envied people. You can recognize them because, despite the humor, the comments feel hostile or spoiling.

For the person with extremely low self-esteem, when someone else feels good about something it can become unbearably painful (**Group 6**). To see other people engaged in happy, loving relationships may give rise to agonizing jealousy. They may avoid the company of such people in order to escape those painful emotions. This might mean isolation, or surrounding themselves with people who evoke neither envy nor jealousy

Feelings of remorse may also become unbearable; because of their brutal, perfectionistic expectations, men and women who struggle with shame may abruptly lose all sense of self-worth when they make mistakes or accidentally hurt someone else. In their own view, they quickly become worthless and contemptible when confronted with mistakes. While they sometimes become defensive, they more often attack themselves for their failures.

In contrast, heavily defended narcissists may try to *inspire* the painful feelings of envy, jealousy or guilt in other people. They provoke envy and jealousy in others not only to convince themselves that they've got it all, but also to rid themselves of such painful feelings. "Showing off" types of behavior where the person seeks to flaunt a possession or attribute often represent projections into the spectator, who must then carry all the unwanted emotion (**Group 5**).

Narcissists can't bear remorse and must always be right. Such individuals frequently try to make their partners, family members and friends feel guilty in a pervasive way, as if to indict their characters: *You should feel really bad about yourself because you're such an awful person.*

Self-Esteem

This entire chapter has focused on the issues of shame and self-esteem. Although I've discussed the three primary areas of concern exclusively in relation to people identifying with **Group 5** and **Group 6** statements, many readers will likely see themselves to a degree in these descriptions.

EXERCISES

Because shame is such an excruciatingly painful experience, you may find this exercise more than usually difficult. It will likely arouse even more resistance than some of the other exercises.

If you have a hard time finishing, be sure to come back to it later. Under no circumstance should you skip this exercise.

1. Try to recall a moment when you felt a flash of humiliation—sudden and unpleasant heat in your face and scalp. You might have looked away or felt unable to maintain eye contact; you might even have wanted to disappear. These physical symptoms express the feeling of shame.

   • What happened to make you feel that way? Did it seem as if something had just been revealed about you that you didn't want other people to see?

   • Describe what you believe was revealed. Did you feel that something negative about your character or your overall quality as a person had been exposed?

2. Are there people in your life who make you feel bad about yourself in comparison to them—not because of things they say

or do but simply because they exist? What is it about them that causes you to feel this way?

3. Do you think in terms of the winners and losers in life? If so, how do you identify yourself, as winner or loser? How do you define "winning"? How do you feel about those people in the *other* group?

4. The next time you go to a party or some other social function where you meet someone new:

   • Pay close attention to the way you introduce yourself. Most of us want to put our best foot forward, but if it goes beyond that – if you notice that you're leaving out a big part of the picture and trying to make your life seem much better than it is – then the entire truth may feel embarrassing or shaming. It's one thing to keep sensitive information private; it's another to present a view of oneself so sanitized that it becomes a kind of lie.

   • What did you leave out? Imagine telling that very thing to someone you've just met. How would it make you feel to tell it? How do you imagine the other person would react to what you had said (even if he or she were to hide that response)?

   • Listen to the way other people describe themselves. You might meet someone who makes her life sound *amazing*, or who tries hard to appear as if she's got it all. How does that person make you feel about him or her? About yourself? Do you struggle to ward off feelings of inferiority? Does envy come up?

5. When you get into arguments with friends, co-workers or partners, how difficult do you find it to admit you're at fault or in the wrong? Most people find this quite a challenge, so don't be too hard on yourself.

- See if you can remember an instance where you were pointing the finger at someone else but had the nagging sense that maybe you were the guilty party. Were you?

- Can you understand why it felt so important to be right? What was at stake and how would you have felt accepting responsibility?

- Have you ever lied to cover up something you felt ashamed about, and maintained an indignant defense of your innocence? What would have been revealed about you had the truth come out? Beyond getting "caught" or being punished, did you fear that exposure would have been humiliating?

6. Do you ever feel contemptuous or scornful?

- Try to remember several occasions when you felt that way about other people or what they did. Write them down.

- Take that list of occasions and see if you can isolate a personality trait or quality from it that strongly evokes feelings of contempt.

- What is it about that particular trait that bothers you so much?

- Can you think of any occasions when you possibly demonstrated this trait? Try hard! Is there anything about yourself you really despise?

7. Do you have a savage inner voice? If so:

- Write down all the things for which it criticizes you. What are its expectations?

- Describe the person you'd be if you were to live up to those expectations. Is that person ideal or without flaws?

- Imagine that you *are* that savage inner voice rather than its victim. Try to identify a feeling of contemptuous superiority, looking down upon flawed humanity (*i.e.,* the *other* you). Does it make you feel strong? Does it make you feel like a winner?

Now What?

You should now have some general idea of the role shame plays in your emotional life and the defenses you use to ward it off: (1) wanting others to pay attention, envy or admire you; (b) blaming; and (c) contempt.

Shame goes along with the recognition that we are damaged; having now completed all the chapters in this middle part and hopefully uncovered some unexpected things about yourself, you may find that shame comes up more than it used to do. You might believe you have more problems than you originally thought and fear that you'll never change.

Don't feel discouraged. The next part will teach you how to work with this new knowledge, to recognize your defenses in action and learn to disarm them. Also bear in mind that everyone struggles with emotional pain, everyone relies on their defenses to ward it off, and few people are brave enough to look inward and challenge those defenses.

You've come this far and that speaks to your courage. On to Part III.

PART III

Disarming Your Defenses

TWELVE

The Mindset for Change

The price of freedom is eternal vigilance.
– Thomas Jefferson

Even if I have explained the various psychological defense mechanisms well enough and you diligently applied yourself to the preceding chapter exercises, you might be feeling a bit overwhelmed. Your customary self-concepts may have received a thorough shaking. My hope is that you won't think about yourself or other people in quite the same way from now on: once you become attuned to the role of psychological defenses in protecting us from pain, the world of human psychology and relationships seems far more complicated.

Richer, too. More textured and fascinating.

Unlike self-help manuals that teach a specific technique for coping with a particular issue, this book aims to enlarge your perspective, to make you a bit of a psychodynamic psychotherapist yourself. In order to benefit fully from your new understanding, you must try to apply it regularly, every day. You need to pay attention to the ways you react and defend, to the emotional challenges that come up for you and the characteristic ways you respond to them.

In working through the chapters and exercises in Part II, you should have developed a sort of internal map, not fully detailed yet but with markers for your primary areas of psychological concern.

How you feel about the experience of being needy or dependent.

Your ability to cope with strong emotions.

The sensitive places that give rise to shame.

You should have a basic sense of the defense mechanisms you typically find most effective in protecting yourself from pain.

The Tenacity of Your Defenses

These defense mechanisms will not go away or disappear simply because you've come to recognize them. They're mental habits developed over your lifetime, "etched" into the neural connections and pathways in your brain. The more powerfully entrenched the defense, the more deeply etched those neural pathways. I like to think of defenses as deep ruts in a well-traveled road. Whenever you travel upsetting terrain, you'll tend to fall into those ruts — that is, you'll use the same old defenses — just as a wheel will slip into an actual rut.

To stay out of that rut, you either have to alter the emotional terrain or figure out a different way to navigate it. Even when you develop other techniques — laying down new ruts, so to speak — the old ones will always pose a problem because they've been around much longer, with years of heavy traffic to dig them deeper.

Always.

As I discussed in connection with shame, if the primary caretakers are severely limited in their ability to provide the emotional nutrients an infant needs, its brain will develop in abnormal and lasting ways. It follows that the personality and defense mechanisms of someone who grew up in such an environment will carry the vestiges of that early experience *for life*. You can't cure it with drugs that rectify a so-called chemical imbalance because the brain's anatomy has been permanently altered. You can't triumph over it by learning a set of affirmations or cognitive behavior techniques, although these methods may offer a genuine kind relief.

This does not mean that authentic change is impossible. My therapist often told me that you can never get rid of anything in your psyche; you can only grow and develop other aspects of yourself to compensate for it. Through insight and hard work, you can forge new neural connections that will offset, at least in part, the damage that has been done. Recent studies in neuroplasticity have revealed the brain's remarkable ability to continue growing and developing throughout adulthood.

The mindset for genuine and lasting change begins with accepting that a cure or total transformation is impossible. Only by coming to know yourself very well, to recognize your trouble spots and the characteristic ways you cope with them, can you start to grow. Only then can you develop new skills and capacities that help you better navigate your emotional world.

Vigilance

You also need to pay attention to yourself, as much and as consistently as you can. In his famous quote at the start of this chapter, Thomas Jefferson was referring to the need for political vigilance to protect hard-won freedoms, but the rule applies to psychological and emotional freedom, as well. You will never become indifferent to the emotional challenges you find most difficult. You will never triumph over shame and permanently leave it behind you. When the usual triggers set you off, your first reaction will be to defend against them in the familiar old ways.

Only by being vigilant–paying consistent attention to yourself, observing your usual defenses in action and then choosing *not* to engage in them whenever possible–will you be able to ease their hold upon you. Only by making a different choice, *over and over*, will you begin to develop new habits. As Sigmund Freud and the many psychodynamic theorists since have come to understand, insight is not enough. The *aha!* moment feels powerful during a psychotherapy session, enlarging the way we understand ourselves, but it doesn't automatically lead to change. Authentic change depends upon the *choices* you make, over and over, throughout your lifetime – the subject of the next chapter.

Like any skill, cultivating the ability to pay consistent attention takes time. You hone your skill through regular effort, just as you become a better musician with daily practice.

Sources of Distraction

You won't be able to recognize your defenses at work if your attention is consistently focused on something other than yourself. Modern life is so full of distractions that we can spend virtually our entire day without looking inward. Career and family life necessarily demand a great deal of our attention, but an endless list of possible diversions awaits to keep us from self-inquiry.

Facebook

The music on your iPod

TV shows and movies

The news

Twitter

Surfing the web

Escapist fiction

Emails and texting

Shopping

The demands of work

Your life partner

Everyone needs entertainment; we all rely on some type of recreation to restore spirits exhausted by the stress of daily life. You need to clear a space between those necessary diversions and the unavoidable demands upon our attention.

In a way, distraction itself is a defense mechanism. By continually distracting ourselves with TV, music, email and the Internet, we divert our attention away from what we'd rather not know. We drown out our pain with a great deal of sensory noise. The mindset for change means cultivating a space of quiet within that noise and tuning into your emotions.

Anesthetics

In addition to deflecting attention away from our feelings, we can also numb them with legal and illegal substances. You might think of drugs and alcohol as supplementary defense mechanisms that alleviate pain when our internal defenses aren't up to the job. As with distraction, we all need to take our minds off our troubles from time to time, and these anesthetics may help you do so. Over-reliance upon them makes it almost impossible for you to develop more effective coping strategies because awareness of the pain has been eliminated.

Without being told, most of us know whether our drug or alcohol use is excessive and we'd be better off reducing it. If you have the occasional nagging doubts, if you imagine that other people disapprove, or if you feel defensive when someone makes a joke about the subject, pay attention. You don't necessarily need to become a non-user, but if you consistently numb yourself and your pain, you make it impossible to learn better ways to cope with that pain.

The mindset for change means reducing your reliance upon drugs or alcohol, enough so that your pain and the defense mechanisms you use to cope with it will come into focus.

Mindfulness

In recent years, the practice of mindfulness, or mindfulness meditation, has risen in the public awareness. Originally described in Buddhism as one of the seven factors of enlightenment, mindfulness has subsequently been incorporated into Western psychology as a method for alleviating a variety of mental and physical conditions, including anxiety and obsessive-compulsive disorder.

Buddha recommended that we establish mindfulness in our day-to-day life by maintaining a *calm awareness* of our bodily functions, sensations, emotions, as well as our thoughts and perceptions. As an aspect of meditative practice, you typically focus your awareness on some particular bodily experience (usually your breathing), gently refocusing attention on it whenever you realize that your mind has wandered away. According to Buddhism, the eventual goal of such a meditative practice is a kind of enlightenment, where emotions such as anger and hatred have been overcome and are absent from the mind.

Because my own experience has taught me that anger and hatred are inevitable, universal aspects of the human experience, I view this goal of mindfulness as highly idealistic. At the same time, I find the *techniques* of mindfulness invaluable as an adjunct to the work I do, with both myself and my clients. Some of my clients have found a meditative practice to be of use, but more of them have eventually decided to do as I do—return, at various times throughout the day, to an awareness of my breath, at the same time attempting to disengage from or silence the mental flow of thought-words.

Especially for people who use "thinking" as a primary defense (Chapter Ten), or who rely on blaming to ward off feelings of shame (Chapter Eleven), it's easy to become immersed in the flow of mind-words and be swept along by it. We're so completely "inside" the process of verbal thinking that we don't even realize it; turning to our breath at various times throughout the day effectively pulls us out of the flow and gives us some distance from it, enough to perceive the words flowing instead of being swept along by the current.

Try it right now. After reading this and the next paragraph, put the book down and focus intently on your breathing. Feel the rise and fall of your chest. Notice the different ways your nostrils feel as air goes in and out of them. (Mine feel cool as I inhale and then warm as I exhale the heated air from my lungs.) Expand your awareness to include other places in your body, noting your sensations. If you're seated, you might feel the pressure of the chair against your back. If there's a breeze, you might notice how it feels against your skin.

See how long you can maintain this quiet awareness before you find yourself distracted by thoughts in your head. Upon their first attempts at mindfulness, clients often report that only two or three breaths go by before they're once again engaged in verbal thought. It's actually quite difficult to do. When you notice that your attention has wandered away from your breath, bring it back to your chest or nostrils, gently disengaging from the flow of words. You haven't failed so do not criticize yourself!

The goal is not perfect mindfulness, but rather an enlarged awareness of our sensations, along with some perspective – that is, some *distance* – from the thought stream that normally sweeps us along. At moments, we may lift ourselves out of that current; from the river bank, we observe our thoughts flowing by, one after another. It's impossible to remain mindful at all times, of course, but creating even a few moments of mental quiet during the day will have its benefit.

*   *   *

As part of the mindset for change, you'll need to incorporate this kind of mindfulness into your daily routine. Even if you choose to buy one of the many excellent books on mindfulness meditation and establish a daily practice,[23] of more importance will be the ongoing process of returning to your breath throughout your daily routine. At first, it may be for merely a breath or two, several times throughout your day. As with all such efforts, you'll get better with practice.

Even if you're not a defensive "thinker," returning to your breath will increase your self-awareness and put you more in tune with your

---

[23] See, for example, Thich Nhat Hanh. *The Miracle of Mindfulness: an Introduction to the Practice of Meditation* (Boston: Beacon Press, 1999) or Smalley and Winston. *Fully Present: the Science, Art and Practice of Mindfulness* (New York: Da Capo, 2010).

bodily sensations. For many people who don't always know what they're feeling, this process of redirecting attention away from their heads and into their bodies helps them begin to identify their emotions.

"Locating" Your Feelings

To state an obvious but possibly unrecognized truth: all human emotion involves "physiological arousal, expressive behaviors, and conscious experience."[24] In other words, when we feel something, we may be *aware* that we feel it, we might *do something* (smile with happiness, for example, or frown with displeasure) and we will experience *bodily sensations* that typically go along with that feeling. Whether we actually *notice* those sensations is a separate issue; if we do not, then we will remain unaware of our feelings: we may frown without realizing it.

In my practice, working with clients who have little contact with their emotions, I often help them to become aware of what they feel by teaching them how to "read" the places in their body where they may register emotion, to recognize the sensations that typically signal a particular feeling. Mindfulness helps facilitate this process. By redirecting attention away from our heads and into our bodies, we're in a better position to recognize the ways that we feel.

When I feel sad, for example, I usually notice the following sensations.

Eyes: even if they don't well up with tears, they'll feel more sensitive.

Mouth/Throat: an achy sensation at the back of my throat; my mouth waters.

Chest: tightness or even pain, maybe a shortness of breath that becomes quivery.

Belly: an unsettled or even queasy feeling.

[24] David G. Meyers. Theories of emotion. In *Psychology,* 7th Ed. (New York: Worth Publishers, 2004), p. 500.

You may not experience it the same exact way, but your sad sensations will likely show up in the same places. Anger shows up in my jaws and temples; my back and shoulders will tense up; I may experience heat throughout my face and upper body. You will likely "find" your anger in the same places.

We begin by cultivating mental quiet, directing our attention away from the distractions of daily life, out of our heads and into our bodies, where we might then notice what we actually feel. Don't decide in advance what you will or will not find once you start tuning in. Be prepared for anything.

Don't Believe Everything You Feel

On the other hand, just because you feel a certain way, it doesn't necessarily follow that the emotion is a reliable guide to objective truth. Whether you're idealizing a new flame and the infatuation feels compelling or you're full of contempt for the idiocy of an acquaintance or you're outraged by the insensitivity of a family member, you don't necessarily have to put your faith in that feeling.

This may seem like odd advice from a psychotherapist who just finished offering guidelines for how to locate your emotions; but while one of the goals of therapy and self-exploration must be to get in touch with our feelings, we sometimes need to maintain a degree of skepticism about them. In the heat of the moment, the intensity of our emotions makes them seem so undeniably *true* that we rely upon them to determine our actions, often to our detriment.

The mindset for change means both getting in touch with difficult and painful feelings and also remembering that sometimes those feelings might be defensive in nature. I'll have more to say about this subject in the next chapter.

Open-Eyed Honesty

Throughout our lives, we receive many messages about the kind of feelings we *ought* to have toward other people. From the first books that our parents read to us, through grade school and continuing into our adult lives, we're taught to be generous, to feel loving, grateful, tolerant of difference, forgiving and non-judgmental, etc.–all the feelings and attitudes that make it possible for a liberal society to thrive. In short, we receive continual instruction in the *correct* way to feel.

It might possibly make society an easier (though less interesting) place if we always felt loving and tolerant toward other people, but in truth, human beings aren't that consistently nice. As I have insisted throughout this book, less socially acceptable emotions such as anger, hatred, jealousy and envy are an indelible part of our emotional makeup. The mindset for change means accepting that you can't avoid those feelings; the best you can do is learn better ways to cope with them as they arise.

Don't expect yourself to transcend or get rid of those painful feelings once you notice them, either. You are not in the process of becoming a more enlightened, nicer person who no longer struggles with these issues; you're trying to develop healthier ways to cope with difficult feelings when they inevitably come up. If you believe that you don't ever feel angry, envious or jealous, then you are lying to yourself in one way or another.

In other words, try to focus on and accept "what is" rather than striving toward what you feel "should be."

Courage and Compassion

If defense mechanisms are lies we tell ourselves to avoid pain, it's because we're afraid of feeling that pain. Of course we are! Especially when we don't know how intense it will be and how long it will last, to face rather than evade pain can be terrifying. If we're to understand and develop more effective ways to cope with it, however, we will eventually need to face our pain. Doing so takes courage.

The mindset for change means mustering your courage but also respecting your limits and not pushing yourself beyond what you can bear. Just as good parents do for their children, you'll need to balance compassion with expectation: on the one hand, don't let yourself back away from an emotional challenge too easily; on the other, don't drive yourself too hard. Be brave when pain begins to emerge but don't force yourself to take on more than you can endure. Like all other skills, developing this kind of endurance takes time. You don't have to face your pain all at once.

Preparing to Choose

To sum up, putting ourselves in a state of mind where change becomes possible involves accepting a number of difficult truths and developing certain mental habits. First of all, we have to accept that our defense mechanisms don't go away simply because we recognize them; struggling with them will be an ongoing challenge. In order to meet that challenge, we need to minimize distractions as much as possible while honing the ability to pay closer attention to ourselves and our bodies.

For change to be possible, we need to be vigilant and brave, balancing firm expectation with compassion for our limits. We need to accept the inevitability of ugly or painful emotions and remain skeptical about the validity of some other feelings that might be defensive in nature. Like good scientists in search of the truth, we must be prepared to accept whatever we may find.

And once we uncover new truths—that is, when we identify a defense mechanism at work and feel the pain behind it—we then must decide *what to do about it*. Insight and self-awareness don't take away our difficult emotions. Instead, they replace reflexive, unconscious attempts to escape from pain with the possibility of choosing a different, more effective response. In the next chapter, I'll discuss the role of choice in disarming your defenses.

THIRTEEN

The Role of Choice

Faced with a choice between changing one's mind
and proving there is no need to do so, almost
everyone gets busy on the proof.

– John Galbraith

Once you recognize that one of your defense mechanisms is at work – that is, once you become consciously aware of it – you have a decision to make: whether to continue with what comes readily and automatically to you or to struggle for change. Choosing to do something different and then following through on your decision takes great effort. Think of that wheel traveling along the rutted road, the ongoing attention and energy needed to prevent it from slipping into the familiar old groove.

In our struggle to change, we will likely come up with new lies in support of the old ones, new reasons to stick with our familiar defenses. Each time we try to talk ourselves out of change, we'll once again be faced with an important choice – to believe the new lie and slip back into the rut or to struggle onward. Meaningful change involves continual choices, difficult ones that will stretch us psychologically and emotionally.

Let me begin with an example that doesn't involve a defense mechanism per se but which should make clear the difficulties involved in striving for change, at least to all of you who have ever tried to lose weight. It helps to illustrate how we often undermine ourselves when we challenge familiar ways of being.

It's Friday, day three on your diet, and you're feeling deprived. The needle on the scale hasn't budged yet; you have doubts as to whether this particular diet is right for you, whether it will actually work, but you soldier on. In mid-afternoon, a friend at work invites you to join her and some other colleagues for a drink at day's end. It sounds like fun, a treat in the midst of all this deprivation. Alcohol isn't a part of your diet, but you tell yourself you can order a Diet Coke instead.

At the local bar, it's happy hour. Your friends go to the buffet table, returning with plates full of buffalo wings and popcorn shrimp. You sip your Diet Coke, nibble on the carrot sticks you brought from home and feel hungry. That margarita your co-worker ordered looks *so* good. As they finish their first round of drinks, your friends all seem in good moods while you feel increasingly grouchy.

You finally decide that complete deprivation, under these circumstances, is really too much and is undermining your resolve. It will actually *help you* to stay on your diet if you let yourself have a drink. How many additional calories could that actually be? You can make up for it tomorrow by cutting back on something else. So you order one of those delicious margaritas and immediately begin to feel better. It goes down surprisingly fast. The tangy aroma of those buffalo wings exerts its pull; almost before you know it, you've made the decision to break your diet—it's clearly the wrong diet for you—and you're heading to the buffet table.

Let's review what happened, the various choice-points you faced and the lies you told yourself. You're very sneaky in the way you undermine yourself: you don't decide to abandon your diet straight away but instead, you chip away at your ability to exercise good judgment.

Happy hour with your friends will be a treat, in the midst of all this deprivation.

Poor Choice No. 1. While it might be a treat, you're also placing yourself in an environment full of additional challenges that will make it all the harder to stick to your diet. When you tell yourself you will be content with a Diet Coke while your colleagues are having mixed drinks, it's a lie.

Going off your diet "a little bit" will help you stick to it.

Poor Choice No. 2. Deciding to have "just one" drink, in order to minimize the sense of deprivation ignores the fact that alcohol reduces our capacity to make good judgments. You secretly know you're on the way to abandoning the diet altogether but you don't admit it to yourself. Instead, you undermine your commitment with a margarita. Without quite admitting it to yourself, you know you're much more gullible when you drink.

This is obviously the wrong diet for me and there's no point in sticking to it.

Poor Choice No. 3. By this point, after downing that margarita, you'll believe just about any lie you tell yourself. You abandon your diet and go back to your old ways, eating the foods you know you should avoid and having another drink because, after all, it's Friday!

Resistance to Change

Attempting to disarm your psychological defense mechanisms and do something different from what you've always done is something like going on a diet. While it would be easier if we whole-heartedly longed to change and grow (or to lose those excess pounds), in truth, we cling to our old habits and resist a challenge to the status quo. At the very least, setting aside a defense mechanism is frustrating, a kind of deprivation like forgoing the foods you always eat. More likely, it involves feeling some pain that the defense has helped you avoid.

You may want to do it, but don't really want to do. As a result, you'll feel the very strong urge to abandon your resolve and slip back into your familiar defenses, just as the person struggling to lose weight feels an ongoing urge to go off his diet. That defense mechanism has protected you from pain; it's unlikely you will whole-heartedly embrace that pain all of a sudden.

Because you're facing the unfamiliar, feeling something new and probably painful, you may also be afraid. Change is scary. It may seem as if facing the unconscious involves more pain than you can bear. In your effort to disarm your defenses, you face repeated choices – whether to move forward and confront that pain or slip back into the familiar old rut. The part of you that fights change will urge you to make poor choices, coming up with new lies to support the old ones.

The degree to which you change will depend upon how honest you can be with yourself, how skillful you become at detecting the internal lies and, as a result, making better choices. Let me give an example of how this process might work.

The More Difficult Choice

Nicole, one of my clients, often slips into a state of denial in which she believes herself to be a remarkably competent person who can handle just about anything when in fact, she can easily become overwhelmed and fall apart if she doesn't respect her limits. She'll come to see herself as an amazingly effective person and begin to take on more and more, eventually overloading herself.

It's a kind of narcissistic defense against awareness of the ways she was profoundly damaged by her childhood (there was a family history of psychosis on both sides) and the shame she feels about the limitations imposed by that damage. Under emotional pressure, her thoughts become increasingly disjointed and out of control; she may develop mild visual or auditory hallucinations and eventually find herself unable to sleep.

In our work together, Nicole and I have gone through this cycle many times: the denial and insistence that she's "just fine," then the emotional mess when she falls apart under pressure because she has taken on too much. After the crash, Nicole may become depressed and feel that she's a complete disaster, a total loser beyond repair. She may feel hopeless about herself and her future...until she gradually recovers and denial again kicks in.

One busy day, Nicole tuned into her thought process and realized she was doing what she had so often done before—attempting to convince herself to take on even more. She had an hour break in her schedule—just enough time to fit in a quick trip to Costco. She felt a surge of energy, propelling her into the "highly competent" mode. Because she works late on that particular day of the week, she usually tries to scale back plans for dinner and prepare something simple. As she felt herself shifting into Super Nicole mode, she recalled that complicated new recipe she wanted to make. She could pick up most of what she needed at Costco then stop at her local market on the way home. Her husband and children would be so impressed!

By that point, Nicole knew herself well enough to recognize what was going on, to identify all the lies she was telling herself. At the same time, it felt so good, experiencing herself as Super Nicole, ready to conquer the world. It felt awful to face her limitations, to accept that she was not a person who could easily fit a trip to Costco into her schedule and prepare an intricate meal after a long day at work. She so much wanted to be that winner who could do everything!

Nicole faced a choice. Fitting a trip to Costco into an already busy schedule would be stressful for anyone, but especially so for Nicole because she tended to fall apart under stress. Would she revert to denial and her narcissistic defenses, believing herself to be that highly competent winner; or would she take into account her damage, her limitations and the shame that went along with them in order to make a better choice? The verbal argument went on within her.

*Sure, you **used** to have trouble getting overloaded but you've grown so much since then. Now you really can handle that trip to Costco. And as for dinner, you're going to be cooking anyway—what's an extra 20 minutes?*

Nicole so much wanted to believe her lies…but she didn't. She chose to remain in her office during her break, resting and reading, instead of going to Costco. Rather than make an elaborate meal, she stuck with the simple pasta dish she'd planned.

As a result, she felt a lot of emotions she didn't want to feel. Anger—that she couldn't become Super Nicole. Shame—that she had so many limitations due to early emotional damage. Grief—that she would never completely transcend the past. To choose such painful feelings over the high of hyper-efficiency demanded a lot of strength and courage. It wasn't easy. She resented having to accept reality. But because she made a better choice, she didn't crash and burn, or slip into depression as a result.

Since then, Nicole has now and then opted for her defenses instead. Change is an ongoing process, and not entirely linear: sometimes you manage to face your pain, on other occasions you slip into the old rut. After years of my own therapy and a lengthy career as a psychotherapist, I still make poor choices. As with Nicole, my old defense mechanisms are always there, calling to me; when life becomes especially challenging or painful, I will sometimes revert to them. I continue struggling in my effort to develop new ruts, better modes of coping, and to face the truth about myself as much as I can.

So don't expect perfection. You're not going to change all of a sudden and then never go back. You can't forever erase or transcend certain parts of yourself, as much as you'd like to. Change is an ongoing process; authentic growth means accepting the relentless nature of our defenses and the ways we continue lying to ourselves. Along the way, we will face one choice after another—whether to go with our defenses or strive to get out of the rut. The choices will never stop.

Once again, let me make an analogy to the practice of a musical instrument. You're never finished learning that instrument; you must continue to practice and to work at it. If you do, you'll continue to improve. If you slack off, your skills will get rusty. But you don't arrive one day at a state of completion and then get to go on permanent vacation.

Like me, Nicole plays the piano. She works very hard at it but with a lot of tension; she feels driven to "get there," to become the polished musician she longs to be, and as a result, she pushes herself too hard. With enough effort, she believes she will arrive at a state of completion, a superior state akin to Super Nicole. In our work, I continually emphasize to her that she needs to love the practice as well – the hard work and ongoing challenges – rather than viewing it as merely a means to an ideal end.

You'll never be finished with change. You'll never arrive at the "new-and-improved" you who no longer needs to struggle. As you go on, you'll continue to face additional challenges, feeling a pull to cope with them in the old familiar ways. As a result, you'll confront one choice after another – to go with your defenses or try to cope in a different way. If you maintain the mindset for change and choose well, at least some of the time, you will continue to grow throughout your life.

Facing Shame

Another one of my clients has struggled with unbearable shame for most of his life and has relied on the typical defenses against it described in Chapter Eleven. In particular, Stan relies on blaming as his primary mode of defense. In his thoughts, he often rants against his wife whenever they have a disagreement. He'll mentally complain about her behavior with a sense of grievance. This has been a life-long pattern in his relationships. Behind his defensiveness, Stan has struggled with the sense that he's emotionally damaged in a fundamental way as a result of his childhood – in other words, with a sense of basic shame as discussed in Chapter Eleven.

During the economic downturn that began in 2008, Stan suffered some reverses in his business that placed a great strain on his family, largely shifting the financial burden of supporting them onto his wife's shoulders until he could recover. She didn't criticize him for what happened nor complain about the weighty responsibility she now had to carry. She recognized that the economic downturn wasn't his fault but Stan nonetheless felt humiliated and defensive. It tapped into a lifelong conviction that he was damaged and ineffectual, a loser.

Two years or so into the downturn, still struggling, Stan noticed that his wife had become increasingly moody. Even the smallest things seem to set her off; when they re-connected after work at the end of the day, she instantly launched into an account of all the things that irritated her about her job. She struck him as quite angry, though not directly with *him*. Because he felt ashamed about his inability to contribute financially as much as his wife, he tried to be supportive and a good listener; it was the least he could do. All the same, he found these "bitch sessions" increasingly difficult to bear.

On a weekend before one of our Monday sessions, Stan and his wife spent much of their free time taking care of chores they used to farm out in financially better days – mowing the lawn, cleaning the house, etc. His wife was in a "bad mood" nearly the entire time. Though he kept it to himself, Stan was ranting about her in his thoughts, complaining about her moodiness and the way she couldn't seem to keep anything to herself.

Stan and I had already been working together for some time; by that point he knew himself fairly well and eventually recognized his blaming defense in operation. After an intense internal struggle, he chose to work hard and quiet his mind, stilling the flow of defensive thought-words in order to create some mental space. There, within this quiet, he found the familiar shame, fueled by that painful sense of responsibility for having brought his family to this difficult place. After all, it was due to his financial reverses that they could no longer afford a twice-monthly house cleaner and the gardener who used to mow their lawn.

Then, with a kind of insight made possible by having disarmed his defense, Stan realized that his wife's complaints and moodiness were her way of expressing the anger she felt about the difficulty of their lives — anger *at him*, in spite of what she had repeatedly said about not holding him responsible. He felt a surge of empathy: in middle age, just when she hoped things would have become less stressful and more financially secure, she had to work harder and with greater anxiety about the future.

On Sunday evening, Stan sat down with his wife and told her what he thought she was experiencing. "As much as you know it's not my fault," he told her, "you're still angry with me." He said it in a straightforward, sympathetic and non-critical way. She immediately acknowledged that it was true. Thereafter followed a long conversation in which they came together as a couple and talked about their future in a constructive way. His wife felt understood. Stan felt relieved. Nobody was to blame for anything.

As I've talked about the need to disarm our defenses in order to face the pain behind them, I might have sounded like a stern parent, telling you to take your medicine simply because it was good for you, but this example demonstrates the potentially large benefits of doing so. Though Stan's blaming defense might have warded off his painful sense of shame in the short term, facing that shame enabled him to empathize with his wife and engage with her in a much more constructive way that brought them closer together.

It also gave rise to a genuine feeling of self-esteem. In our Monday session the next day, Stan told me he felt proud and grateful for his ability to understand himself and his wife in these ways, to respond constructively rather than defensively, with compassion instead of criticism. The residual shame that goes along with early damage might never leave him, but he found it could live side-by-side with feelings of pride for the hard work he'd done in order to grow and for what he could now accomplish. He found the entire experience deeply moving.

As paradoxical as it may seem, the path to building authentic self-esteem depends upon accepting the reality of shame and choosing not to defend against it.

Justifying Our Defenses

The two examples given so far involve people who identified a defense mechanism at work by listening closely to their mental process: Nicole "heard" the lies she was telling herself in order to deny her own limitations. Stan eventually recognized the defensive nature of his internal rant, how he *blamed* his wife in order to avoid his own shame. By "thinking," they each tried to convince themselves of the validity of their defenses.

As I mentioned earlier, this internal effort to persuade ourselves that our defensive perspective is "true" is one of the hallmarks of a defense mechanism. It is repetitive and insistent. If you tune in and listen closely, it will actually *feel* defensive, as if you're arguing with someone in order to convince him or her that your own point of view is the correct one. Even though no one has actually challenged you, you will proceed to defend yourself. I sometimes find myself engaged in mental arguments with an actual person I know, a dead giveaway that I'm on the defensive.

Through repetition, this process of self-justification also stirs up emotions that feel entirely real and convincing, especially when it comes to the blaming defense. Both Nicole and Stan could work themselves into a state of righteous indignation that felt quite persuasive. Whenever you feel yourself to be an entirely blameless person who has been wronged, nourishing your wounds in a state of superior innocence, you might want to stop and wonder if something else might be behind it.

Distrusting Your Emotions

In other words, as I suggested in the last chapter, you don't have to believe everything you feel, especially when it comes to emotions stirred up by this internal process of justification. Contempt, righteous indignation and angry blaming may be aroused by our defense mechanisms in order to shore them up. We therefore need to be skeptical about the validity of those emotions.

This is where the breathing and mindfulness techniques discussed in the preceding chapter can be extremely helpful. Especially when self-justification is at work, bringing ourselves to a state of quiet will often lower our emotional temperature. By focusing on our breath, we can take the wind out of feelings impelling us toward some action we may later regret. Stop and take a deep breath. Bring an end (for as long as you can) to the mental chatter. Turn your inner eye on these intense feelings and clear some space for the idea that they may not be entirely valid.

This would also to apply to situations where we have an outsized emotional response to a person or event – when we are "triggered" to use the phrase currently in vogue. We may react with rage (fight mode) if we feel embarrassed or humiliated and deep shame threatens to emerge. We might go into terrified flight mode when our anxiety gets stirred up. In those cases, as well, creating a quiet space in lieu of immediately reacting to strong emotion will allow us to *choose* how we respond.

I don't mean to sound as if this is an easy thing to do. For me personally, it's one of the most difficult challenges I face. It's very hard to remain skeptical in the midst of strong feeling, so much easier simply to "run with" it. Triggered emotions are very difficult to withstand. As with everything, it gets easier to do with practice. Some day while riding the emotional juggernaut, you'll strive for quiet, and recognition will come to you: *I've been here before and I know where it leads. Better stop.*

Feelings Don't Last Forever

When we fall head-over-heels in love, when someone important to us dies and we succumb to profound grief, or if a panic attack suddenly overwhelms us, the intensity of the experience can make us believe we will always feel that same way. Strong feeling seems to defy or negate time; in the midst of it, our entire reality consists of the here and now. We may be unable to think, to let memory guide our expectations for the future, or to use imagination in order to glimpse a time when we may feel differently.

As our defense mechanisms loosen their automatic hold upon us, as we come into contact with the pain we've been evading, we may fear it will last forever. Our first inclination will be to retreat from that pain, reverting to the defense we originally developed to cope with it. While resorting to that defense is the habitual, familiar response, once we become aware that we're doing so, we may *choose* to do something different. Often that means bearing with the pain long enough until it eases or some new feeling arises.

This too shall pass is a proverb that applies both to the impermanence of all material states as well as to our emotions. Infatuation fades and people fall "out of love"; after a painful period of mourning, most people emerge from the most profound stage of grief; a panic attack comes to an end. Caught up in the maelstrom of emotion, however, we may find this almost impossible to believe. When we come into contact with the pain we've been avoiding through our defense mechanisms, we may fear that it will overwhelm us.

You might recall a time when you felt this way as a child — overwhelmed by some feeling and convinced it would last forever. Most children feel this way at one time or another. In Chapter Eight, I discussed how babies rely upon projection in order to rid themselves of unbearable emotions; part of the reason they do so is because they have no idea how long those feelings will last and fear they will go on forever. Babies and even older children don't yet understand the transience of experience.

Just as mindfulness and a focus on our breathing may help curtail states of emotion stirred up by our internal self-justification, so may they help us withstand pain that seems endless. Pain has a disorganizing effect on our psyche: because we're afraid, we want to shift our attention away from it – to run from it, so to speak. A focus on our breathing helps us to "re-organize," to gather our attention and attach it to a neutral experience – the rising and falling of our chest, the sensation of air passing through our nostrils. We may even find a kind of comfort in the familiarity of that experience. It helps us to wait long enough for the feeling to ease.

When discussing the issue of bearing with pain on my website, one reader understood me to be saying something like "Just suck it up." I mean nothing of the kind. People who use that expression often do so with impatience or contempt, as if to say "Shut up and quit your whining." Instead, I'm offering guidance for how to bear strong, often painful feelings long enough for them to pass, or for you to figure out how you might address that pain rather than resorting to the familiar defense.

Challenging the Hidden Defense

So far, I've been discussing the sometimes striking ways we're able to spot our defenses at work. What about the hidden defense, the one so embedded in our personality that there may be nothing to "hear," but rather complete silence on the subject of strong emotion or neediness?

The man whose defenses are so successful he never consciously feels anger.

Anyone with virtually no interest in sex.

The woman whose narcissistic defenses are so successful that she doesn't come into conscious contact with her shame.

Disarming these defenses requires a different kind of effort, one where you may need to put yourself into an unfamiliar or even dreaded position that will challenge those defenses. Take the example of the exercise from Chapter Two, where I suggested that you make a point of asking someone else for help. For the person whose character is marked by self-reliance, using the words "I need your help" would likely stir up some uncomfortable feelings that otherwise wouldn't arise.

The calm, phlegmatic character will have learned to avoid situations that might arouse conflict or lead to intense emotion. I'm not suggesting that such people pick a fight in order to feel something, but breaking out of one's comfort zone is essential. If you're uneasy with conflict and stifle your opinions, you might need to risk disagreeing with a friend or relative...about something small, at first. Don't push too hard. Breathe deeply and try to bear with the unpleasant or even painful feelings that come up as a result.

If you have largely repressed awareness of your sexual desires, you may need to recover them by making contact with those parts of your body where you would feel desire: your genitals. In *The Black Swan* (2010), the company choreographer directs Nina, his sexually repressed prima ballerina, to masturbate, pushing her to connect with a part of herself she has disowned. You might need to do the same. In the process, you may confront intense internal opposition – fear, disapproval or disgust (reaction formation). It will take courage and perseverance *not* to retreat.

Let me give a more detailed example from my practice that demonstrates how to go about challenging your character, and the sort of emotions that might come up as a result. My client Erika was a middle-aged woman who had worked for a number of years as administrative assistant to the vice-president of a large corporation. Although highly intelligent and responsible when it came to her job, Erika found it difficult to complete some of the more challenging assignments her boss had tried to give her – the kind of work he would normally have handed over to a junior officer in management. He apparently sensed Erika's enormous potential and tried to develop it.

In our work together, Erika and I explored the reasons why she was unable to complete these assignments. As she began each one of them, she'd find that she couldn't think clearly about the issues and would get mired down in minutiae. The work required close attention to complex numbers, and throughout her life, she had struggled with math.

Eventually, it became clear to us that the assignments actually made her *angry*. She resented the added responsibility; she didn't want to have to think for herself or work so hard. As a result, her mind would go "out of focus" as she became mentally passive.

This passivity was a strong feature of her entire character. Beginning in her late teens, Erika had developed powerful attachments to teachers and other mentors, longing for a special closeness where these figures would look after or "think" for her. As an adult, she relied upon her husband when it came to financial decisions and took little initiative in maintaining their friendships. In a highly active and idealized fantasy life, she imagined herself involved with someone dynamic and powerful; their union would present the answer to all her difficulties and he would then take care of her. Waking up to the reality of her actual life and her responsibility for it often made her angry.

Her hostile reaction mirrored the way she felt about growth in therapy. Whenever we glimpsed signs that she had begun to change, becoming less reliant on my help and more able to use what she'd learned, Erika felt resentful about it. She refused to become independent and take care of herself, retreating to a place of passivity where she would remain forever my "child." She insisted that she was a therapy "lifer" and would never be able to get by without treatment.

Her apparent helplessness actually reflected a kind of stealth control (as discussed in Chapter Nine) with which she tried to evoke a care-taking response in other people so they would do the mental work she resented. In therapy, she viewed me in a highly idealized light, expecting me to think for her, solve her problems and tell her what to do. Although devoted to treatment, she was actually quite passive, leaning upon me to "fix" everything without her having to make an effort.

Due to our ongoing work, Erika gradually began to recognize the price she was paying for her passivity. She was in her mid-50s: time was passing, opportunities were slipping away. She eventually made an important choice, forcing herself to do a number of things she had avoided and didn't really want to do. She taught herself some new financial software and took over the household budget. Next, she enrolled in an accounting course to help with the more challenging assignments at work. At home, she took a more active role in their social life. At the same time, she made a great effort to curtail the idealized fantasy life that contributed to her passivity.

Over time, through her struggles, Erika became much more effective and capable in just about every area of her life. As a result, she felt a number of emotions, some of which took her by surprise. Though she had expected to feel angry about confronting reality as she'd done in the past, she was unprepared for the grief and sense of loss. Like my client Stan, she felt proud of herself for doing this hard work; but seeing her potential—seeing how much she could really do when she put her mind to it—made her feel the years she'd lost by remaining passive. With her native intelligence, what might she have done if she'd exercised her mind instead of expecting other people to think for her?

When defenses become too entrenched for too long, they usually wind up restricting our lives and stunting our emotional growth. Once we stop, we may need to grieve for lost time, missed opportunities and failed relationships. Disarming a defense always involves facing pain.

The Ongoing Nature of Choice and Change

By now, I hope I've made it clear that wrestling with your defense mechanisms will be a lifelong process. If you keep at it, you'll continue to grow and change, but you'll never arrive at a state of completion, the new-and-improved you who no longer struggles with the same familiar issues. At the age of 57, after my own lengthy stint on the couch and a much longer time continuing the work alone after my therapy ended, I still struggle with many of the same feelings on a daily basis. I'm in good mental shape, so to speak, and up to the challenge because I regularly exercise the skills I've developed, but I won't ever consider myself "done."

It's like going to the gym, in a way; once you stop exercising, you'll eventually lose the benefit of all those hours you put in, so you need to stick with it if you're to stay in shape. As I've said before, the process is analogous to playing the piano. In order to make beautiful music, you need to keep your hands strong and agile with regular exercise. For you to lead the most emotionally rich and satisfying life possible, you must keep listening for and observe the cues that signal a defense at work, or challenge the invisible ones embedded in your character..

And when you do, you may then *choose* to react or behave differently. It may not seem like a lot, compared to the wish for a happily-ever-after sort of life free of pain and conflict, but the ability to choose represents one of our most prized freedoms—whether it's the political freedom to choose that is embodied in democracy, or the psychological freedom to manage our feelings and behavior in more constructive ways, once our defense mechanisms no longer dictate our behavior so completely.

F O U R T E E N

The Future of Your Defenses

Idealism is the despot of thought.
– Mikhail Alexandrovich Bakunin

From the beginning of this book, I've described defense mechanisms as a means to ward off pain that we find unbearable. Although I've explained the importance and benefits of sometimes bearing that pain, you might still wonder why you're doing all this hard work, and where the effort of disarming your defenses is supposed to lead. At the end of the day, you might want to ask: *What exactly does mental health look like?*

On the one hand, I'd like to answer that question by leaving as much room for variation as possible. I see "normal" as an ideal that no one achieves. Especially with the rise of mass media and family-oriented sitcoms, our culture has promoted a sanitized view of the well-adjusted individual for whom no conflict causes much pain and whose problems are easily resolved. In truth, all of us (including people who come from reasonably happy homes or have spent years in successful therapy) retain our difficult, sensitive places as well as our defense mechanisms to cope with them. Everyone's life is full of pain, a lot of it, and nobody copes with it perfectly.

On the other hand, I also believe there truly is a kind of mental health that takes into account and accepts the reality of one's human nature, rather than defending against it too powerfully. It might look something like this:

> *You tolerate dependency reasonably well, with an overall sense of getting what you need more often than not.*

> *You feel deeply without fear of being overwhelmed, confident that your emotions give meaning to your life and relationships.*

> *You can trust your sense of who are you; you're not 100% satisfied with yourself, though you **are** certain you're a person of value who hasn't stopped growing.*

Since defense mechanisms don't permanently disappear, even if you understand them, you'll continue to grapple with your defenses in this state of "mental health." They won't look exactly the same as they once did; now that you're conscious of them, they won't control you quite so powerfully. After a long period of honest self-appraisal and a lot of hard work, here's how your defense mechanisms may continue to affect you and play a role in connection with your primary psychological concerns.

Denial and Repression

Because you're more in touch with your needs, you find it much harder to continue for long periods unsatisfied, though now and then, you still catch yourself pretending you're entirely self-sufficient. In a way, it seemed so much simpler, not knowing about all these needs, especially when you have to wait a long time to get what you want. You find yourself turning to substitute emotional resources less than you used to do, but under stress, it's often easier for you to overindulge than to ask for help or set limits for yourself. On the whole you feel a lot more satisfied than before.

Those little oversights and "innocent" mistakes don't seem as harmless as they once did; whenever you realize you've forgotten to do something you promised, you're now in the habit of wondering what you might be angry about. You can't always spot your hostile feelings at first but in the end, you usually do. As much as you don't want to talk about them with your friends and loved ones, you find it usually helps. Not always. Sometimes you wish you had kept your mouth shut.

Though you know better, you still long to believe that human nature (including your own) is less aggressive, "nicer" than it really is, and that the conflict of emotions is avoidable. Sentimental movies about simple good people who eventually go on to live happily-ever-after bring tears to your eyes. You still want to be a "good" person, though you're less sure of what that means. Although you sometimes hate the ways that you feel, you believe it demonstrates strength of character that you're willing to face them.

You still don't believe you're going to die, not really. You prefer not to think about it.

Displacement and Reaction Formation

You don't take things out on other people as much as before. You're better able to identify the actual reasons why you feel the way you do, though sometimes it's scary to face the truth. On those occasions when you're not quite onto yourself and you end up hurting an innocent bystander, you feel guilty in a way that seems entirely appropriate to you. The guilt isn't overwhelming. You do your best to apologize and make up for the hurt you caused.

Some of your responses and opinions have lost much of their intensity. You might still feel that knee-jerk revulsion to some things but because you don't truly believe in it, the reaction dwindles away. Now and then, you feel just as harshly judgmental about someone's behavior as you used to do, but knowing yourself better now, you realize it's only because you badly want to do the same thing, even if you can't quite permit yourself to do it.

You've become a more accepting person in some respects, but that doesn't mean you always approve. No matter how much you know there's a kind of defense involved in your reaction, there are some things you will never like. You're not quite so self-righteous about it, but you see no reason to dig deeper into your disgust for smokers.

Splitting

Although on occasion, you still find yourself insisting, with angry conviction, on what you're certain is true, you've become a more thoughtful person. The world doesn't seem quite so clearly a place of good and evil, of us-versus-them. It's a lot more work to balance differing perspectives and settle for less than absolute answers; sometimes, you long to retreat to your old certainty, but on the whole, you have much more interesting conversations these days. You're careful not to engage too fully with people mired in black-and-white thinking, especially when it comes to politics and religion.

When you feel hatred toward someone you care about, you're better able to keep in mind that you also love this person and not blast him or her with the full force of your rage. Not always. Sometimes you still say and do things you later regret, wishing you could better manage such strong feelings, but you're more inclined to feel remorse than to justify your behavior. Over time, it seems like you're getting better at thinking and feeling at the same time.

Your perceptions of other people and their emotional life have changed, too: everyone seems so complex! You feel impatient with dogma, political or otherwise, that tries to manipulate you and inspire hatred for some other group. Sometimes you're completely disgusted with the simple-minded good-us/bad-them mentality that permeates politics.

If you don't have a committed relationship and want one, you're on your way to finding it. You don't fall in and out of love as you used to do; you know what you're looking for and you're willing to tolerate less than perfect, so long as you can feel genuine love and concern amidst the difficulties. In all your intimate relationships, you're less "touchy" than before. You can tolerate other people's anger, at least when it's not deliberately hurtful, and you don't feel that admitting to error is a grave humiliation. You're only human, just like everyone else.

Idealization

Your lows aren't quite so low as before, but your highs aren't as high, either, and you're not completely happy about that. You still wish there was a way to maintain that heady *life-is-wonderful* feeling at all times without having to suffer through the down days, but you reluctantly accept that one is linked to the other. There are no perfect, final answers to your difficulties. You know that happily-ever-after occurs only in fairy tales and romantic comedies.

Your love for romantic comedies might be as strong as ever. When one of your friends falls in love, you still feel a twinge of envy, even if you know this blissful infatuation can't last. Alcohol and recreational drugs still have the power to inspire that same kind of high. You may struggle with your habits; every once in a while, you might end up imbibing more than you had intended and feel the worse for it the next day.

You're not so convinced of the absolute goodness of your heroes, and you now believe that even the bad guys have some redeeming qualities. Sometimes, you wish things were simpler than they are, and it's hard to resist nostalgia for a mythical time when things appeared to be simple. As much as you know better, it's difficult to believe that your favorite celebrities don't have vastly more interesting and emotionally satisfying lives than your own. If you're not careful, that unacknowledged belief can make you bitter.

Vacations still mean a great deal to you. Even if you know you may be setting yourself up for a disappointment, you still look forward to them with great expectations. Usually, you have a pretty good time anyway and going back to "real life" isn't quite the let-down it used to be. Vacation real estate guides hold just as much appeal, but now you're skeptical that life in a different town or country would be qualitatively different from the one you lead now.

You don't turn on friends, family members or loved ones when they hurt or disappoint you. You're better able to tolerate the frustration that inevitably comes up when you depend upon real, imperfect people. You don't have a lot of friends but you're sure of the ones you do have, warts and all. They've seen your warts, too, and they love you anyway, though sometimes you get on one another's nerves.

Projection

Looking back on those conversations when you used to unload on your best friend, you feel a little embarrassed. It was so inconsiderate, and what exactly did you think you were getting out of it? When people you know do the same thing to you now, the experience makes you very uncomfortable; in as gentle a way as possible, you put an end to it. You try to be clear on the difference between dumping and sharing. When you confide in someone now, you make sure you're talking to the right person, someone whose opinion you value and whose advice you might actually follow.

It's a point of pride that you try very hard not to take your feelings out on other people. Despite your best efforts, on a very stressful day, you may still catch yourself "guilting" someone who made a simple mistake; even if you try, you may not be able to stop yourself. Later, remorse will lead you to apologize. Most of the time, you feel more forgiving toward loved ones who occasionally bite your head off because you understand they're beyond their emotional limits. Except for your cousin—you don't feel forgiving there. He becomes a total jerk under stress and the way he doesn't even try to restrain himself really pisses you off.

Your relationships with friends, family and loved ones no longer seem so lopsided. You don't feel as if you're too needy or that other people depend upon you too much. You've come to value the concept of reciprocity, though sometimes it seems that few other people feel the same way. Now and then, you wonder about some of the friendships you lost over the years, in large part because you couldn't see the other person clearly or expected too much, and you wonder whether that friendship might have survived if you'd understood then what you understand now. It can make you a little sad.

Control

You're reasonably neat: you neither drive your loved ones to distraction with your need for everything to be perfect nor leave your place a mess, hoping someone else will clean it up. While you still become anxious just before departing on vacation, you understand that your significant others may have ideas different from your own about when to leave for the airport and which route to get there will save the most time. They may be wrong, but you don't insist on having it all your own way. Relinquishing control makes you anxious, though in a different way than it used to – less desperate to put a stop to it, less angry at others for getting in your way.

At work, people tell you that you seem more relaxed these days, and they obviously like it. This kind of compliment is hard to hear because it reminds you of your old behaviors, knowing the effect they must have had on your co-workers. You *do* feel more relaxed, though sometimes more helpless. Now and then you have to remind yourself that perfect control of every variable in life is impossible to attain, even though it presents itself to your mind as a viable answer.

The reality of friends with spouses or parents able to provide them with a more comfortable life than your own doesn't get under your skin the way it used to do. As much as it appears that some people

217

get a free ride and are completely taken care of, you don't believe they pay no price. You value your hard-won self-reliance and what you bring to a relationship, even though you will admit to yourself (and no one else) that you still wish somebody would acknowledge all that and say, "Because you've worked so very hard, you can stop trying now. I'll take care of you."

In social situations, you feel much freer and more yourself than before. You don't try so hard to control how others view you, to make it seem like everything is "just fine." Except when that woman from the accounting department gets going about her latest "amazing" dinner party; you understand what she's doing but it still gets to you. You've come to place a deep value on those conversations with close friends, and even on occasion with an acquaintance, when people admit to being in difficulty and you find how much your struggles have in common.

"Thinking"

This is an ongoing issue and you know you'll always need to keep returning to quiet throughout your days, refocusing on the places in your body where you register emotion. The rationalizations aren't such a problem—when you catch yourself in one of them, you usually smile and sometimes turn it into a funny story to tell at dinner that night. When you misbehave, you don't jump on board with your attempts to justify it; you apologize when necessary.

You can still lose yourself in long rambling trains of thought. On days when "thinking" takes over, you might feel alienated from the people who matter most to you, unsure of how to get back in touch with them and with your own emotions. Occasionally you may feel trapped inside your head. Mental silence and a mindful focus on your breath always help you out...provided you remember to try. Sometimes you're surprised at how long you can go, caught up in the mental chatter, unaware that you're doing it.

Even if you know better, you're always drawn to the articulate person who appears to have it all together by virtue of her complete mastery of language. Sometimes a well-turned phrase still seems like a kind of magic. At the same time, you've come to have a much higher regard for the ordinary exchanges of daily life that give it meaning: a dinner with old friends, even if the conversation wasn't scintillating, that bike ride along the beach when you didn't say a word, Sunday morning in the bed with newspapers.

It's definitely more challenging to feel than not to feel; most of the time you don't regret it. When you find yourself locked away in your head for long, it soon begins to seem like a wasteland, so dry and empty of life that you'll long for your feelings, even for your pain. Anything is better than such a desolate existence. Often when you come back to yourself and reconnect with your loved ones, it brings tears to your eyes. You have no words to describe the sense of grief and gratitude – grief for the lost years, gratitude for the life you now enjoy.

Shame and Self-Esteem

You feel much better about yourself, proud of your personal integrity and the hard work you do to make better choices, but from time to time, you may catch yourself "showing off" in ways that fill you with shame. Maybe you've had a couple of drinks and hear yourself describing how impressed so-and-so was with you, or subtly bragging about your latest accomplishment. When you think about it later, you feel embarrassed that the secret longing to be admired or even envied by others is still with you.

The shame you feel is old and familiar, but it doesn't decimate you the way it used to do. You don't savage yourself with recrimination and destroy your sense of self-worth. At the same time, you hate this feeling of shame and wish there was some way to "heal" and be free of it forever. It will always be with you; you can live with that. In a way, knowing that the experience of shame is always a risk puts you on your mettle. You're aware that you still have some narcissistic tendencies, probably always will, and the shame helps keep you humble.

Accepting responsibility for your mistakes comes more easily to you now. A twinge of resentment may fuel the wish to turn the tables when someone criticizes you, but you know better than to do it. You don't have to win every fight. Sometimes contempt will still twist your lips but you rarely believe the feeling is valid. The pain you're trying to ward off isn't always clear to you. It may take hard work to trace a line back from contempt to the source of your shame.

You don't feel as competitive as you did before; you're no longer afraid that you're an envious loser so far beneath the winners who have it all. The world strikes you as quite a different place now. Everybody has pain. All men, women and children have needs they sometimes find difficult to bear. Sometimes it seems that nearly everyone has secret places full of shame, too. Now that you understand the link between shame and narcissistic behavior, you can see the enormous role shame plays in the lives of so many people you know.

On balance, you'd rather be you than somebody else. Of course there are things about yourself you wish you could change. It would be nice if you could catch onto your defensive maneuvers sooner. You often wish you didn't have to fight the same battles every single day, even if the struggle seems much less difficult than it used to do. And of course, you wouldn't mind being younger, wealthier and more attractive.

Despite the inevitable frustration and pain, you take genuine pleasure in so many of your experiences. You cherish your relationships, too, finding a deep sense of meaning in the feelings that connect you to family, friends and romantic partners.

Most of the time, you feel glad simply to be alive.

Conclusion

Much of what I've written in these last pages describes my own mental health – my daily struggles with the familiar ongoing challenges, the ways I've grown and the ways I am still the same person who started therapy nearly forty years ago because he was so depressed. I know myself far better now and I've developed in many ways that mitigate the damage caused by my childhood, but when pain and shame become too much, my old defense mechanisms are still at hand. I try not to rely on them too much.

I've had the privilege of working long-term with a number of men and women who came to me for individual psychotherapy; the same holds true for each one of them, as well. They've all grown enormously. In many ways, they're the same people who came to me years before, asking for relief from their pain. In the course of our work together, they developed a deep understanding of themselves, along with the mental and emotional skills to manage their pain without my help. They can bear feeling needy in their relationships, experience a broad range of emotions and often feel quite good about themselves. None of them is entirely shame-free.

For my clients as well as for me, self-observation has become a way of life. None of us has finished learning about ourselves and as a result, none of us has finished growing. There are still days when I surprise myself, when I recognize some new form of self-deception, encounter pain, but find a way to address it that works much better than my old defense. In the life that I envision ahead of me, I'll continue to feel pain and continue to develop more honest ways to cope with the pain, and that will increase my sense of well-being. I feel good about that.

According to the first of Buddha's noble truths, life means suffering: various types of pain and disappointment are an inevitable part of the human condition. Less philosophically, in *The Princess Bride*, the Man in Black says to Buttercup: "Life *is* pain, Highness. Anyone who says differently is selling something." Nowadays, the pharmaceutical industry tells us that psychic pain can be alleviated with the help of a drug, or perhaps a combination of them. This point of view dominates the mental health profession throughout the Western world, resulting in billions of dollars in profit for the companies that sell those drugs. In writing this book, I've attempted to offer a different perspective. I mostly agree with that Man in Black. Life isn't entirely pain, but from my experience, there is no shortage of it. Not for anyone.

The ways we defend against that pain, often to our own detriment, has been my subject; enabling you to recognize your defenses at work, disarm them and find more effective ways to address your pain has been my goal. I hope that reading this book will help you find ways to tolerate your needs and fulfill them in your relationships, to experience the broad range of emotions that lend meaning to life, and to feel satisfied with yourself as a person. It will be a lengthy, never-ending process. Following the advice set forth in this book won't erase your pain or forever heal your shame, but if you do your best to follow that advice, the effort will help you to lead a richer, more comprehensible and more satisfying life.

Additional Reading

In important ways, all of the books below influenced my understanding of our primary emotional concerns. Because they're written in the scientific language of my profession, many readers may find it difficult to connect with them on an emotional level; but if you're interested in finding out more, these works lie at the heart of psychodynamic theory as I learned it. Mine is a highly selective and personal list.

W.R. Bion. *Second Thoughts.* (New York: Jason Aronson, 1967).

_____. *Seven Servants: Four Works by Wilfred R. Bion.* (New York: Jason Aronson, 1977).

Sigmund Freud. *The Standard Edition of the Complete Psychological Words of Sigmund Freud.* (London: The Hogarth Press, 1957)

Melanie Klein. *Love, Guilt and Reparation and Other Works,* 1921-1945. (New York: Macmillan, 1984).

_____. *Envy and Gratitude and Other Works,* 1946-1963. (New York: MacMillan, 1984).

Heinz Kohut. *The Analysis of the Self.* (New York: International Universities Press, 1971).

Heinz Kohut. *The Restoration of the Self.* (New York: International Universities Press, 1977).

Donald Meltzer. *The Kleinian Development.* (Perthshire: Clunie Press, 1978).

R.E. Money-Kyrle. *Man's Picture of His World.* (New York: International Universities Press, 1960).

D.W. Winnicott. *Through Pediatrics to Psycho-Analysis.* (New York: Brunner/Mazel, 1992).

_____. *Maturational Processes and the Facilitating Environment: Studies in the Theory of Emotional Development.* (London: Karnac Books, 1996).

Acknowledgments

During my freshman year in college, profoundly depressed and struggling in my courses, I made an appointment with a psychiatrist in Beverly Hills. At the time, I knew nothing about psychotherapy or psychiatry; I'd heard this man's name from my father, a contractor, who mentioned him as an investor in a building project. I had no idea where else to turn and didn't mention the appointment to my parents. After the psychiatrist met with me, he convinced my father of my need for treatment and referred me to a colleague he felt could help.

I began once-a-week treatment with Michael Ian Paul, M.D. and stayed with him for the next 13 years, increasing to twice a week after five years, then to three and eventually four times per week once I'd completed my master's degree and began psychoanalytic training. I consider myself a very fortunate man. It was pure chance that the psychiatrist had invested with my father and I happened to hear his name; fortunate for me that he didn't send me to a different colleague. I recognized that I needed help, sought it out and held on tight once I found it, but it was coincidence that my own life circumstances brought me into contact with Michael Paul.

Not a day goes by when I don't make use of something I learned from him; even now, more than 25 years after the end of my analysis, I think of him often and feel grateful for what he gave me. When people I know complain about the cost of psychoanalysis and marvel that I stayed in treatment for so long, I can only answer: "What price do you place on your life?" I worked hard to afford my therapy after my parents refused to pay for it, and I did my best to make use of our sessions; but without his help, I wouldn't have my family, my career or the friends I enjoy today.

Without my experience as Michael Paul's patient, I could never have written this book. So many of the insights these pages convey were absorbed and assimilated during my years on his couch. I learned how to be a therapist largely by witnessing his fine example. I express myself in different ways, perhaps, and my understanding of shame evolved long after the end of my analysis, but my views of human nature and what drives us are essentially the same as his.

During formal psychoanalytic training, I had excellent teachers and supervisors, and I learned from them as well. Richard Alexander, Robert Caper, James Gooch, Yvonne Hansen and Donald Marcus all played an important role in my professional development. The friendship of my classmate Tom Grant sustained me through training. I'm also grateful for the trust and loyalty of my clients, many of whom stayed with me for years, often waiting for my understanding to evolve enough so that I could help them.

When I moved to Chapel Hill, North Carolina 14 years ago, good luck brought me to Laurel Goldman's Thursday afternoon writing class. Laurel is the most sensitive, insightful critic I have ever met. Along with my fellow classmates Christina Askounis, Angela Davis-Gardner, Peter Filene, Linda Orr and Peggy Payne, Laurel helped me to grow as a writer. Chapter by chapter, I read the first versions of this book during our class; the group's critiques and encouragement helped shape the book you're reading today.

Almost two years ago, Marla Estes suggested I write a series of posts for my website, detailing the different defense mechanisms; it was her idea to write a book about how to "defuse" one's defense mechanisms. As the book unfolded, it became something much larger, a more comprehensive outline of the human experience and an attempt to adapt what I'd learned as a therapist to the self-help format, but credit for the original idea goes to Marla. Melissa Kirk of New Harbinger Publications suggested the title.

My good friends Kathy Stanford and Dave Birkhead brought their graphic design skills to bear on cover art and book design. Without

Michael Eha's relentless support and encouragement, I could never have completed this project.

Finally, I want to thank everyone in my family for their patience and enthusiasm—especially my son William, who long ago urged me to start blogging.

About the Author

Joseph Burgo, Ph.D. has practiced psychotherapy for more than 30 years, holding licenses as a marriage and family therapist and clinical psychologist. He earned his undergraduate degree at UCLA and his masters and doctorate at California Graduate Institute in Los Angeles. As an instructor, he has taught graduate students in psychology and supervised their training in community counseling centers. He is also a graduate psychoanalyst and has served as a board member, officer and instructor at a component society of the International Psychoanalytic Association.

As a writer, he has published two novels, both works of genre fiction released some time ago and now out of print. He formerly wrote a column on parenting for a small syndicate of newspapers in the Los Angeles area and helped devise content for the World Bank's website, the Development Gateway. He currently writes the popular blog *After Psychotherapy* where he discusses personal growth issues from a psychodynamic perspective. In addition, he writes a blog entitled *Therapy Case Notes*, hosted by PsychCentral, where he discusses issues that arise during individual psychotherapy sessions.

In his private practice, Dr. Burgo provides face-to face internet video counseling and psychotherapy to clients in the United States and Canada, as well as in Europe, Africa, and Asia.

Made in the USA
Monee, IL
05 October 2020